P9-DGH-843

DISCARD

EXISTENTIALISM, FILM NOIR, AND HARD-BOILED FICTION

EXISTENTIALISM, FILM NOIR, AND HARD-BOILED FICTION

Stephen Faison

CAMBRIA
PRESS

AMHERST, NEW YORK

Copyright 2008 Stephen Faison

All rights reserved
Printed in the United States of America

No part of this publication may be reproduced, stored in or introduced into a retrieval system, or transmitted, in any form, or by any means (electronic, mechanical, photocopying, recording, or otherwise), without the prior permission of the publisher.

Requests for permission should be directed to: permissions@cambriapress.com, or mailed to:
Cambria Press
20 Northpointe Parkway, Suite 188
Amherst, NY 14228

Library of Congress Cataloging-in-Publication Data

Faison, Stephen E.
    Existentialism, film noir, and hard-boiled fiction / Stephen Faison.
        p. cm.
    Includes bibliographical references and index.
    ISBN 978-1-60497-573-4 (alk. paper)
    1. Film noir—History and criticism. 2. Detective and mystery stories—History and criticism. 3. Existentialism. I. Title.

    PN1995.9.F54F35 2008
    813'.087209384—dc22

2008040359

This is dedicated to my parents and friends whose loving support of my efforts has been unwavering. This book would not exist were it not for the kind, constructive, and enthusiastic encouragement of John Lachs.

TABLE OF CONTENTS

ACKNOWLEDGMENTS

I am grateful to so many people whose support and encouragement made it possible for me to accomplish this book. The staff personnel at the Philosophy Department and Graduate School at Vanderbilt University confirmed their deserved reputation for expertise and professional service. My colleagues in the Philosophy Department offered invaluable constructive criticism that helped to strengthen the book.

Time will not permit me, given the finite duration of my life, to adequately thank John Lachs for his patient guidance and friendship. I can state without hyperbole that without his wise and loving advice and counsel, this project would not have been undertaken, much less completed. John immediately and enthusiastically supported the philosophical value of my enterprise, and encouraged me to pursue my passion for the subject. I always left John's company, and that of his beautiful wife, Shirley, feeling cared for and appreciated.

During the years of learning and writing, my energy was nourished by the delight and pride over my modest accomplishments felt and expressed by my father, Neal III, and siblings, Neal IV and Kathy. My perseverance was sustained by the memory of my mother, who before her passing said, "I always knew you were smart," and my grandmother, who had the foresight to refer to her inquisitive little grandson as "professor." I am morally required to confess that the term was not always intended as a compliment.

Finally, I am much obliged to the staff at Cambria Press for their genial stewardship of the publishing process. They cracked the whip with steady, gentle hands.

EXISTENTIALISM, FILM NOIR, AND HARD-BOILED FICTION

COMING TO TERMS WITH FILM NOIR AND EXISTENTIALISM

"Let's get the details fixed first."[1]
—Sam Spade to Caspar Gutman in the film
The Maltese Falcon (1941)

The alleged official arrival of existentialism to the United States was marked by the much publicized visit of French existentialists, Jean-Paul Sartre, Albert Camus, Simone de Beauvoir, and Maurice Merleau-Ponty to New York soon after World War II. Newspapers and popular magazines, aware of the American fascination with French culture, focused much of their attention on the personalities of companions Sartre and de Beauvoir, and the fashionable trend of the movement back in Paris. The American press reported a virtual cult following for existentialism among young Left Bank bohemians, who were conspicuous by their black garb and heavy makeup, chain-smoking, enthusiasm for night-clubs and American jazz, and their talk of meaninglessness and despair.

The titles of novels and plays like *Nausea, The Stranger, Journey to the End of Night*, and *No Exit* contributed to the notion of existentialism as pessimistic, fatalistic, and nihilistic.

These perceptions contributed to the chilly reception French existentialism received from the American academic philosophical community. American intellectuals were skeptical about whether existentialism was a philosophy at all. It was criticized as excessively morbid with its themes of alienation, anxiety, and the absurd, and it was dismissed as the psychological expression of the French war experience. Furthermore, its leading representatives seemed like literary artists and popular celebrities more than *serious* philosophers. Existentialism was considered one of those French fads, and it was felt that the American public's curiosity would no doubt fade with the emergence of the next fad.

The prevailing view is that existentialism had no significant presence in the United States before the 1940s.[2] After all, it was only introduced by the French after the war, and the fad was evaluated and then dismissed by the popular press and ignored by the intellectual community. Moreover, existentialism's pessimistic outlook was considered contrary to the American optimistic mood. France came out of World War II a shattered and defeated nation, its soil occupied and riches plundered by the Nazi enemy. The United States emerged from the war victorious and poised to begin a period of national prosperity and world ascendancy. Americans had every reason to feel confident about the direction of the nation and optimistic about their personal future. It was understandable that the French would embrace a philosophy that expressed their experience, but Americans had little reason for despair.

In this book, I argue that conventional wisdom about existentialism in the United States is mistaken. Its presence in this country was overlooked because existentialism was treated as a European phenomenon that had to be introduced to the United States, and then it was largely rejected because its values were considered contrary to the American ethos. I will demonstrate that the United States developed its own unique brand of existentialism at least several years before Sartre and Camus published their first existentialist works and more than a decade before their famous visit to New York. My position is that film noir and the hard-boiled fiction that initially served as its source material represents one distinctive form of American existentialism and that this form was produced independently of European philosophy. What is unique about American noir is its exploration of existential themes of absurdity, contingency, meaninglessness, and despair from the perspective of working-class men. French and American intellectuals agreed that Americans had no sense of despair, but the commercial success of American noir undermines that assessment.

I do not contend that other analyses of hard-boiled fiction and film noir are untenable, but I submit that the dominant themes expressed in these works lend themselves most easily to existentialist interpretation. In this book, my role as philosopher is to make explicit the implicit existential metaphysical, epistemological, ethical, and political meanings conveyed in the narrative forms of fiction and film.

Through my discussion of American noir, I expect to accomplish a couple of objectives beyond establishing American noir as one form of existentialism. I intend to describe and celebrate the production of a kind of existentialism by and for working-class people. As I use novels and films to make my case, I mean to illustrate that philosophical ideas are available from a rich diversity of sources. Furthermore, I submit that philosophers do themselves a disservice when they restrict what is called *existentialism*, or *philosophy*, to that which academia traditionally approves. The tendency to limit the range of sanctioned material led the professional community to miss the philosophical importance of the critically acclaimed phenomenon known as film noir. I also mean to show that by restricting the sources of philosophy, we limit the discussion of philosophical matters to elites, ignore those outside the university system, and contribute to the class divisions that required working-class Americans to create their own existential vision.

What is sometimes called *American noir* begins with hard-boiled crime fiction and the cycle of Hollywood films made from these stories. The case for the existential value of American noir will be made, but it is immediately clear that early examples of hard-boiled crime fiction precede the introduction of French existentialism, since these stories appeared during the 1920s. The visiting French philosophers agreed that American soil was not fertile for existential thought. Americans were not alienated, had no pessimism about human nature, and lacked the necessary anguish about the problems of human existence. As is often the case, these intellectuals overlooked certain segments of the population that potentially were most anxious, alienated, and pessimistic. American noir was first written for and by members of the working class, and this portion of the public was evidently receptive to its existential content.

Noir is generally recognized as *film noir*, the retrospective title given to a cycle of crime films made in Hollywood during the 1940s and 1950s. *The Maltese Falcon* (1941) and *Touch of Evil* (1958) are usually considered the first and last films of the cycle.[3] The French title literally means *black film*, and French writer Nino Frank is often credited with coining the term because of the resemblance to the *Serie Noire* crime novels popular in France at the time. These black and white films are remarkable for their distinctively dark visual style, disorienting camera angles, convoluted narratives, morally ambiguous characters, and bleak outlook on life. The film noir cycle, though popular with general audiences, received scant attention from academics in the United States until the growth of film studies programs in the 1970s.[4] Since then, a virtual cottage industry has developed around these films.

Though existential themes are sometimes attributed to certain noir titles, these comments are typically only stray remarks that fail to explore and analyze the existential content of these films and their literary source material. As if to justify scholarly examination of Hollywood crime movies, attempts were made to provide film noir with a respectable pedigree, and it should come as no surprise that the artistic merit was attributed to German (expressionism), French (poetic realism), and Italian (neorealism) influences. So film noir is often described as though it were a European phenomenon that astonishingly occurred on American soil.

Since film noir appeared during the 1940s, film scholars use developments during that decade to explain the emergence of the cycle. By the

1940s, many German-trained professionals were employed in Hollywood. These immigrants are usually credited with injecting German expressionist techniques into the visual style of Hollywood crime films. A less assertive claim about European influence is made for the narrative style and content of the movies. Though hard-boiled fiction is acknowledged as one source, film noir is often defined as primarily a visual style. This account is useful to advocates of European influence because it de-emphasizes the American source material. To the extent that existentialism is mentioned, the reader is left to assume the European origin, as though any material of intellectual value could only have come from Europe.

Robert G. Porfirio's refreshing 1976 essay, "No Way Out: Existential Motifs in the *Film Noir*," gives the most attention to the relation between film noir and existentialism; his article is one of very few that even mentions such a connection. Porfirio's effort is especially remarkable because he immediately requests that his use of the term *existential* not be too closely tied to the specific philosophies of European existentialists. Porfirio agrees, "[E]xistentialism as a philosophical movement was largely unknown in the United States until after World War II, when the French variety was popularized by the writings and personal fame of its two leading exponents, Jean-Paul Sartre and Albert Camus" (80). So Porfirio reasons that if film noir contains existential motifs, and these themes were not imported from Europe, they must have developed here in the United States. Porfirio explains, "[S]uch attempts on the part of Hollywood to borrow directly from that European tradition would have been rare indeed, particularly in the 1940s. It is more likely that this existential bias was drawn from a source much nearer at hand—the hardboiled school of fiction without which quite possibly there would have been no *film noir*" (82–83).

It was common practice for Hollywood studios to purchase the rights to popular novels and turn them into films, and by the 1940s they had accumulated a stockpile of these crime stories. Porfirio was not concerned to analyze the connection between existentialism and hard-boiled fiction, but that connection is essential to this discussion because hardboiled fiction is the foundation for the existential content of film noir.

American noir begins with the hard-boiled crime fiction of writers like Dashiell Hammett, James M. Cain, Horace McCoy, Raymond Chandler, and Cornell Woolrich. These stories and novels were part of what could be called a literary underworld, and first appeared in pulp magazines and inexpensive paperback books. They were called *hard-boiled* because of their tough and sordid realism and the concise and forthright narrative style that matched the manner of the characters. The outsiders and loners in these stories were the disinherited working-class white men of the 1930s, whose protective (hard-boiled) shell was a defense against a callous world.

Hammett's best known novel, *The Maltese Falcon*, was published in 1930, Cain's *The Postman Always Rings Twice* appeared in 1934, McCoy's *They Shoot Horses, Don't They?* was released in 1935, and Chandler's *The Big Sleep* appeared in 1939. These four novels and other less known titles (including several by Woolrich) mark the beginning of this classic period of noir novels in the United States. The books by Hammett, Cain, Chandler, and Woolrich were made into films early in the noir cycle. During the 1950s, new writers appeared, like David Goodis and Jim Thompson, and the final years of the film noir series involved a greater diversity of characterization.

Porfirio was more correct about the connection between hard-boiled fiction and existentialism than he realized or cared to express. It was highly unlikely that existential themes in film noir were imported from France, but the French existentialists certainly felt the influence of American hard-boiled fiction. In 1946 Horace McCoy was reportedly "hailed in Paris" as the first American existentialist (Madden, *Cain* 171). Not only is the hard-boiled brand of existentialism not indebted to the French, the French actually borrowed ideas from the Americans. Camus was inspired to write *The Stranger* after reading James M. Cain's *The Postman Always Rings Twice*. Camus' first major novel is written in a style similar to Cain's (Cruickshank 16). While much attention is given to the influence of French existentialists on Americans, French observers acknowledged the value of American writers whose work preceded their own.

The Maltese Falcon is considered the first film noir and is one of the great existential novels. Hammett's 1930 book had already been filmed twice by Warner Brothers, under its own title in 1931, and as *Satan Met a Lady* in 1936. The latter was a relatively comic vehicle for Betty Davis. John Huston received permission to direct his first film and chose *The Maltese Falcon*, realizing it had been filmed twice before, because he believed the earlier versions were not faithful to the spirit of the novel. Huston felt that Hammett's story was written in a screenplay-friendly manner, and he left the dialogue virtually intact. Huston's selection of sets and visual style explored the darker side of Hammett's vision without resorting to German expressionistic techniques. So the acknowledged first film noir is clearly not the product of European influence, but it is the creation of an American director determined to remain faithful to the spirit of the work of an American writer.

The film noir cycle substantially begins in 1944, with *Double Indemnity*.[5] Billy Wilder directed the film that was based on the novel by the American writer, James M. Cain. Billy Wilder emigrated from Central Europe and lived in Berlin, and *Double Indemnity* contains several notable scenes associated with the noir visual style. Nevertheless, Wilder took issue with Robert Porfirio when, during an interview, the latter asked about the influence of his personal history and German Expressionism in the director's work. When asked whether his noir films, *Double Indemnity, Sunset Boulevard, Ace in the Hole*, and *The Lost Weekend* were influenced by his personal history, Wilder replied, "No, I honestly cannot point my finger at any small incident, even in those pictures, which would reflect my background, and where I came from" (Wilder 104). In the specific case of *Double Indemnity*, "I just tried to dramatize, Raymond Chandler and I, working on that screenplay, to emphasize what Mr. Cain had in mind," Wilder expressed (Wilder 104).

Study of film noir has quite understandably been the territory of film studies, and their scholars have tended to emphasize cinematic qualities and pay less attention to narrative sources. The failure to give sufficient credit to hard-boiled fiction leaves them with a problem. The 1930s and 1940s were notable for the pressure censors exerted on the studios, which were strongly discouraged from displaying overtly sexual, excessively violent, or anti-American attitudes. Film noir offers a gutter's eye view of America; the nightmare version of the American Dream from the perspective of marginalized working-class men. Those who consider film noir a phenomenon that begins in the 1940s have had a difficult time explaining how Hollywood was suddenly able to exhibit this cycle of films that challenged the production code and depicted the American system and its values as saturated with corruption.

The frequently offered explanation is that the victorious Americans were suffering from their own psychological war wounds during the 1940s. In his seminal essay, "Notes on *Film Noir*," Paul Schrader contends that Americans experienced their own postwar disillusionment. The "acute downer" was a "delayed reaction to the Thirties," he writes (55). According to Schrader, during the 1930s movie content was deliberately upbeat to provide relief from the Depression and divert attention away from the development of war in Europe. Schrader remarks that after the war, the "disillusionment many solders, small businessmen, and housewife-factory employees felt in returning to a peacetime economy was directly mirrored in the sordidness of the urban crime film" (55). After the war, every film-producing country experienced a period of realism in cinema, Schrader notes, and American audiences wanted "a more honest and harsh view of America," that reflected the reality they experienced (55).

Of course, this explanation does not square with the consensus view that during these same 1940s Americans were not receptive to the call of pessimistic existentialism. And the contention that the wartime experience gave Americans a jolt of reality that they now expected in their films does not explain the popularity of the prewar and wartime hard-boiled fiction that served as film noir source material. During the very decade that movies were required to be cheerful, hard-boiled fiction writers were producing pessimism that sold very well. Schrader calls the "acute downer" of the 1940s a delayed reaction to the Depression of the 1930s, but hard-boiled fiction actually begins during the 1920s. If Schrader is correct, general audiences were prepared by the war for the dose of realism offered by film noir, but since its initial source material, in the form of hard-boiled fiction, was popular before the war and the Great Depression, evidently some American audiences were already prepared in the 1920s for this realism.

The 1920s are notable for the Lost Generation authors, including F. Scott Fitzgerald and Ernest Hemingway. George Cotkin in his *Existential America* contends that the Lost Generation writers "enunciated a metaphysical condition of despair and alienation," which "embraced an essentially existential perspective" (24). These authors expressed the disillusionment felt by a generation who, Fitzgerald wrote in *This Side of Paradise*, had "grown up to find all Gods dead, all wars fought, all faiths in man shaken" (282). Lynn Dumenil's examination of Fitzgerald's work in *The Modern Temper* reveals that "beneath the glamour of his flappers and jazzhounds lay a fragility rooted in their failure to find meaning or purpose amid the uncertainty of modern life" (150). Hemingway's first novel, *The Sun Also Rises* (1926), features a lost cast drifting aimlessly, their instability symbolic of their homelessness and inability to find substance in the modern world.

Hemingway is appreciated by some to be the father of the hard-boiled tradition, and it can be argued that writers like Hammett and Chandler were taken more seriously because their styles were considered similar to his. Hemingway was recognized as a literary artist, a title only recently accorded to Hammett and Chandler.[6] Hemingway's link to the hard-boiled tradition is mostly due to his tough prose and the tough characters depicted in his writing, but Hemingway did not write crime stories. *To Have and Have Not* (1937) is the novel most related to hard-boiled fiction, and the only one that actually contains criminals. Two of his short stories, "The Killers" and "Fifty Grand," feature hoodlums, though only briefly in the latter tale.

The Lost Generation writers offer an existential perspective that begins during the 1920s, and might be called *a rich man's existentialism*. Their characters are mostly members of the leisure class, who live in a decadent world of vanishing illusions. But another brand of existentialism was brewing during this decade, and its characters do not suffer from disillusionment because they harbored no illusions.

According to Paul Schrader, film noir emerges because audiences desired greater realism in their films. An increasing number of postwar moviegoers considered films depicting "the seamy side of things" to be a more accurate representation of their experience of the United States. A similar movement occurs in detective fiction with the shift from Golden Age mystery writers, like Agatha Christie, Arthur Conan Doyle, and Ellery Queen, to the hard-boiled tradition. Raymond Chandler describes this development in his essay, "The Simple Art of Murder." According to Chandler, a significant segment of mystery readers were dissatisfied with Golden Age detective stories and wanted more realistic crime fiction. These readers "were not afraid of the seamy side of things: they lived there" (Chandler, "Art of Murder" 989).

The original consumers of American noir read their tough-guy detective fiction in pulp magazines like *Black Mask*, where Hammett and Chandler published their early stories. Dumenil explains that pulp writers identified with their readers and saw themselves "as workmen who produced piecemeal prose for people like themselves" (31). Chandler credits Dashiell Hammett with starting the realistic hard-boiled tradition because Hammett "took murder out of the Venetian vase and dropped it into the alley" ("Art of Murder" 989). In other words, "Hammett gave murder back to the kind of people who commit it for reasons, not just to provide a corpse; and with the means at hand, not hand-wrought dueling pistols, curare and tropical fish (Chandler, "Art of Murder" 989). Furthermore, Hammett did not write in the elevated prose of the Victorian era, but in "the American language," the speech of "common men" (Chandler, "Art of Murder" 989).

American noir was the creation of writers who toiled at their labor, assembling stories for as little as one penny per word. Pulp writers were about the business of creating fiction that would appeal to the genre's mostly working-class readers. Out of this initially modest ambition, they created the noir world. Hammett and Chandler did not create, but refined, the hard-boiled detective, whose existential approach enables him to survive in the doomed world he must negotiate to earn his meager living. His world, life, and philosophy represent the essential themes of existentialism for the common man.

The noir detective is presented as a member of the working class, whose lonely struggle is to make an honest dollar in a dishonest world. His cynical amorality is conditioned by the contradiction between the nation's expressed principles and the cold, cruel reality. In hard-boiled fiction and film noir, the trail of clues generally leads from working-class subordinates to the rich and powerful who veil their criminal activities behind a cloak of respectability. The hard-boiled detective may solve the case; that is, he may discover *whodunit*, but he cannot stop the deterministic forces that operate behind the scenes. He cannot control the cards he is dealt, but as an existentialist, he insists upon the freedom to choose how he will play those cards.

Existentialism is an outlook that begins with the individual's psychological and moral disorientation. It emphasizes contingency in a world without transcendent values or moral absolutes, a world devoid of any meaning except that which the individual creates. Existentialism has its positive aspects of freedom, responsibility, and authenticity. The creators of American noir, writing from the perspective of the estranged working class, were drawn to the negative aspects of existentialism characterized by alienation, anxiety, meaninglessness, and death. The titles of noir-ish films often express these negative features. *Caught, Cornered,* and *No Way Out* illustrate the disorienting sense of entrapment. *Detour, Suddenly,* and *Street of Chance* describe the uncertainty and danger of contingency. *Kiss Tomorrow Goodbye, Kiss Me Deadly,* and *Kiss of Death* communicate that even a most tender expression can be fatal. *Nightmare, I Wake Up Screaming,* and *In a Lonely Place* articulate the anxiety, fear, and alienation of the noir world. *Force of Evil* and *Touch of Evil* attest to the unsettling feeling of hidden, malevolent powers.

Our inability to explain human existence is demonstrated by the futility of activity in the noir world. The resolution of the noir detective's case usually settles very little and leaves him wondering whether the whole affair was worth the bother. In *The Maltese Falcon* the object of the quest, "the stuff dreams are made of," turns out to be a fake. In *The Big Sleep*, the catalyst for much of the chaos is a murder that finally no one cares about. *The Asphalt Jungle* began a subcategory of heist-noir, in which a team of working-class professionals is carefully assembled to commit an intricately planned robbery. Though in heist-noir the theft itself is usually accomplished, unforeseen and incalculable consequences unravel its aftermath. The failure of these activities demonstrates that human beings cannot control their world, and their endeavors are ultimately futile.

The existential mood of noir is depicted by the bleak imagery of a physical world filled with stark, barely lit interiors, shadowy corridors and alleys, and rain-soaked streets that Chandler described as "dark with something more than night" (Introduction to "Art of Murder" 1016). The isolation of the individual and the lack of transcendent values are personified by the noir protagonist, who is typically a cynical, morally ambiguous loner without conventional standards of ethics. Thrown into incredibly dangerous situations by the randomness of existence, miscalculated actions, or the requirements of his profession, the protagonist is forced to play a high-stakes game to its bitter conclusion. In *D.O.A.*, a vacationing accountant learns that he has been fatally poisoned for notarizing an incriminating bill of sale several months ago. In *Detour*, a piano player hitchhiking to Los Angeles is involved in two accidental deaths, and though he is not guilty of murder in either case, at the end of the story, he wanders the highways grimly anticipating his inevitable capture by the authorities. In *Double Indemnity*, a critically wounded insurance salesman staggers to the office during the wee hours to dictate the fatal consequences of his willing participation in a murder. As these narratives unfold, the characters are left to ponder and explain to what extent they are responsible for their conditions. In American noir, the existential attitude is not so much chosen as realized, as circumstances force protagonists to examine their lives.

Attention must be given to the fact that American existentialism was not produced in the ivory towers of academia but instead emerged in genre fiction and Hollywood films. American philosophers not only failed to produce a version of existentialism but failed to notice its presence in the form of noir. Part of the problem is that existential meaning is obtained through the encounter with the vicissitudes of life rather than by contemplation of abstractions, as the individual is jolted into recognizing the reality of his or her condition. Consequently, the best presentations of existentialism are found in creative works that present characters in extreme situations. The narrative approach used in literature and film is better suited to existentialism, but academic philosophers tend to value systematic explications and sometimes fail to treat the content of popular fiction and movies as legitimate sources of philosophy.

Academia's failure to recognize this uniquely American brand of existentialism can also be traced to the professionalization of philosophy and the evolution of the definition of *philosophy*. Philosophy began as love and pursuit of wisdom but, over centuries, developed into an academic occupation. The autonomous sage became the philosophy professor, a scholarly specialist whose duties consist of the study and teaching of specific thinkers and texts, and the logical analysis of selected problems or language complexities. Philosophy became a university endeavor with its own insular world of authorities writing mostly about matters of interest to experts in language too obscure for most nonprofessionals. This development created a moat around the ivory tower between academics and the public and produced a sharp distinction between what is considered philosophy and what is not. Canonical texts and academic writings are philosophy; fiction and movies are not.

While academic philosophers were discussing abstract ideas of limited interest to those outside the profession, American genre writers and filmmakers produced existential fiction and films that responded to their audiences. The same novels and films that slipped the notice of American philosophers were critically acclaimed in France (the proclaimed birthplace of existentialism), where intellectuals did not observe our artificial borders between disciplines. It is more than ironic that existentialism, which criticizes traditional philosophy as "academic, superficial and remote from life," was produced in the midst of American philosophers who were too disconnected to notice (Kaufmann 20).

I argue that hard-boiled fiction and film noir represent an American existentialism, but the terms *existentialism* and *film noir* have been notoriously difficult to define and the subjects of much disagreement among academics. The debate over meaning has become tiresome, especially as it pertains to film noir, and I do not pretend to offer a perfect solution to this problem, but I am obliged to clarify how I will use the terms in the following chapters, and explain why certain definitions are unsuitable.

TERMS OF ENGAGEMENT: EXISTENTIALISM

Some philosophers and commentators describe existentialism as a shared mood articulated by creative writers such as Fyodor Dostoevsky, Albert Camus, and Franz Kafka. Others insist it is a systematic philosophy best expressed in methodical works such as Jean-Paul Sartre's *Being and Nothingness* and Martin Heidegger's *Being and Time*. The systematic works are sometimes described as responses to what John Wild refers to as "The Breakdown of Modern Philosophy" in *The Challenge of Existentialism* (see ch. 1) During the twentieth century, traces of existentialist thought were retrospectively discovered in the writings of Soren Kierkegaard and Friedrich Nietzsche, and these figures are often cited as protoexistentialists. In any case, existentialism is presumed to be a European phenomenon defined by its most visible and outspoken representative, Jean-Paul Sartre. Sartre offered "existence precedes essence" as a concise definition of what he called existentialism, effectively planting the flag of Europe in the soil of the unnamed and therefore unclaimed frontier (*Existentialism* 13).

European existentialism, in its familiar French versions, appeared in the aftermath of traumatic national, continental, and world events that challenged the ontological, epistemological, and ethical claims of modern philosophy. In "Situation of the Writer in 1947," Sartre explains how the atrocities of World War II shook the foundations of prevailing moral assertions:

> Chateaubriand, Oradour, the Rue des Saussaies, Dachau, and Auschwitz have all demonstrated to us that Evil is not an appearance,

that knowing its cause does not dispel it, that it is not opposed to Good as a confused idea is to a clear one, that it is not the effect of passions which might be cured, of a fear which might be overcome, of a passing aberration which might be excused, of an ignorance which might be enlightened, that is can in no way be diverted, brought back, reduced, and incorporated into idealistic humanism…(178).

Sartre's words depict a world in which the rational order is in question, where human beings are capable of the unspeakable and incomprehensible.

In a book that is often credited with introducing existentialism to American readers, *Irrational Man*, William Barrett explains that existentialism begins with "The Encounter with Nothingness," and he devotes a subchapter to this topic (see ch. 2). The abyss was expressed by Albert Camus as the unbridgeable gulf between man's desire for metaphysical assurance and his inability to find that assurance with his religious beliefs and philosophical systems. The absurd, as Camus described the phenomenon in *The Myth of Sisyphus*, "is born of this confrontation between this human need and the unreasonable silence of the world" (28). In Camus' account, and those offered by most European versions of existentialism, the absurd confrontation assumes cosmic proportions, as the universe itself is the source of human frustrations. Barrett places the conflict at a more terrestrial level and identifies the decline of religion, the rational ordering of society, and the rise of science and the idea of finitude as the developments contributing to this encounter with nothingness. Stripped of the certainty provided by religious beliefs, humans are left with nothing, abandoned and forlorn, without meaning or purpose, in a world indifferent to human endeavor. The rational ordering of society replaces the paternal Christian God with the bureaucratic state, and authority becomes less predictable and accessible.

Certainly the encounter with nothingness is not limited to postwar Europeans. Each culture defines and expresses its own existential engagement, just as the Europeans did theirs. The existential outlook is not the exclusively property of any culture; therefore, I will employ a generic definition of *existentialism*. The purpose of this book is to discuss the phenomenon of noir in fiction and film, which I contend is a manifestation of one form of existentialism in the United States. There is enough resemblance between fiction and films I will describe and European versions to account for usage of the same term, but too close a connection may oblige us to judge the American noir experience by the European standard, a condition I wish to avoid. Existentialism is a shorthand term for a compelling vision of the world that is at least as old the ancient Greek dramas. Secondly, existentialism's criticism of Western philosophy noted by Walter Kaufmann resembles that made by American philosopher John Dewey. In Dewey's 1917 essay, "The Need for a Recovery of Philosophy," he chastises Western philosophy for prioritizing the abstract problems of philosophers over the concrete problems of people (230). Unfortunately many of the attempts to characterize existentialism as a systematic philosophy responding to the breakdown of modern philosophy suffer from the same deficiencies.

Because I will present film noir as a form of American existentialism, an applicable source for defining existentialism is the *American Heritage Dictionary*. This neutral reference defines existentialism as "a philosophy that emphasizes the uniqueness and isolation of the individual experience in a hostile or indifferent universe, regards human existence as unexplainable, and stresses freedom of choice and responsibility for the consequences of one's acts." (642). Employing this definition, I am free to explore this uniquely American version of existentialism without emphasizing European models.

My presentation features chapters that discuss the existential metaphysics, epistemology, ethics, and politics of noir, but these terms will not be used in the service of analysis of abstract concepts. In fact, existentialism is critical of traditional philosophy's attempts to reduce existential questions to abstractions for the purposes of intellectual manipulation. Existential questions are often ignored because they resist such attempts. I will discuss these terms in the larger context of philosophy as love and pursuit of wisdom as guidance for living. In this book, metaphysical, epistemological, ethical, and political challenges arise out of the protagonist's difficulties in the world.

My discussion of the existential metaphysics of noir does not offer a theoretical inquiry into *the nature of reality* but expresses the often harrowing experiences of the randomness of existence, the accidental and coincidental, the existential expansion and contraction of time and space, and the presence of "fate or some mysterious force" (Al Roberts in *Detour*). The existential epistemology of noir does not present an abstract analysis of *the problem of knowledge* but pertains to insurmountable barriers encountered by desperate seekers of concrete information. These obstacles are especially common to the private detective's search to find out *whodunit, whodunwhat* and how and why they *dun* it. The epistemological question is not *how is knowledge possible?* The protagonist asks, "How can I find out what I need to find out?" given numerous concrete barriers. The existential ethics of noir do not compare theories of moral values or search for the supreme principle of morality, but examine noir's irredeemably corrupt world in which conventional standards of morality are obsolete and irrelevant. In the realm of noir, only a saint or fool is ethical in such a wicked world; nevertheless, protagonists are reluctant to conclude that all is permitted. The existential politics of noir do not engage political theories but trace film noir's critique of the cleavage between the nation's expressed values and its actual practices. In hard-boiled fiction and film noir, the encounter with nothingness does not have cosmic origins, nor does it pertain to the breakdown of modern philosophy, but it emerges out of the emptiness of a corrupt society.

In summary, this book is not the basis for an abstract inquiry into the nature, causes, or principles of reality, knowledge, and values. American noir, in the form of fiction and film, does not attempt to prove the truth of propositions pertaining to the isolation of the individual in a meaningless world or the unexplainable nature of human existence, but it offers a compelling vision of the world in which these conditions are experienced by human characters in concrete situations. The world is revealed as meaningless, not in some abstract sense that the universe cannot provide meaning, but in the sense that the metaphysical, epistemological, ethical, and political limitations of the noir world crush the goals, objectives, and actions of protagonists, leaving them to realize the futility of their endeavors. As he surrenders to police in *The Killing*, Johnny Clay sums up the failure of his intricately planned robbery with a shrug, and mutters, "What's the difference?"

Terms of Engagement: Film Noir

Though there is general agreement about the origin of the term *film noir*, there is considerable disagreement about whether film noir is a genre, style, or cycle. Unfortunately, these classifications matter if for no other reason than because they affect which films are admitted to the canon.

Genre advocates contend that film noir has common features just like other genre films. After all, they claim, that is how one knows one is watching a film noir. Westerns typically present characters in cowboy hats and boots, with pistol belts and six-guns, a sheriff or marshal, a rancher or farmer, a doc, and a tinhorn. They feature a town with a saloon, a livery stable, a jail, or they are set at a ranch, wagon train, cattle-drive, or cavalry fort. These iconic symbols immediately cue the viewer that a Western is in progress. Noir films, genre advocates argue, contain certain noir-ish characters such as the femme fatale, the private detective, the victim of circumstance, a crew assembled for a heist, etcetera. These films include urban mean streets and back alleys, the detective's austere office and apartment, the shabby hotel rooms, the slick nightclubs.

Style advocates contend that certain cinematic and narrative characteristics distinguish film noir. Narrative devices include first-person voiceovers, flashback reports, nonlinear scene sequences, convoluted plots, and unresolved endings. Visual features include oblique camera perspectives, deep-focus photography, low-key lighting, and tightly framed compositions. These techniques contribute to the shadowy, unstable, and dangerous atmosphere of film noir. Some style advocates point out that these methods can be applied to a comedy, horror, or science fiction film. If the style position is accepted, film noir is not limited to a specific historical period, nor is it restricted to crime films.

Cycle advocates consider film noir a series of crime films that appeared between 1940 and 1959. They clash with genre and style advocates over the acceptable period of film noir. While cycle advocates tend to agree with style advocates about the narrative and visual features of noir, they insist that by the end of the 1950s the cycle had run its course. The studio sets and artificial lighting common during the 1940s that gave the films their distinctive look gradually yielded to location photography, monochrome visuals, and more natural lighting during the late 1950s. Early noir films present activity from the point of view of the criminals, or the private detective, but during the 1950s, the emphasis gradually shifts to the perspective of the police investigation.

There are problems with each of these definitions. While wardrobe and setting are enough to identify a film as a member of the Western genre, the visual cues for film noir are less definitive. Presences of a mystery, private detective, or duplicitous woman are not enough to label a movie film noir; nor are criminal activities and seamy locations. There are plenty of movies with these features that do not qualify as film noir, such as the Sherlock Holmes films starring Basil Rathbone. The style position is inadequate because it dismisses the origin of the term, which was originally created for the wave of crime films that first appeared during the 1940s. If any film with dark photography, unusual plot twists, and an ambiguous ending is allowed, including comedy, the definition of film noir is stretched to the point of meaninglessness. Even some cycle advocates contribute to this problem because they seem willing to admit almost any suspenseful melodrama released within the accepted range of years. Furthermore, if film noir is a cycle limited to the 1940s and 1950s, we are left with the problem of classifying later films like *Chinatown* (1974) and *The Grifters* (1992), which seem to contain all the elements of film noir except black and white cinematography.

These definitions are so liberal that almost any film can qualify as noir. As a result, hundreds of movies are now classified as film noir, and the list continues to expand. Alain Silver and Margaret Ward edited the first comprehensive guide, *Film Noir: An Encyclopedic Reference to the American Style*, published in 1979. The third edition (1992) boasts more than 300 films from the classic period, then adds another 49 *overlooked* titles in an appendix. By 2003, Michael Keaney had identified more than twice the total offered by Silver and Ward in his *Film Noir Guide: 745 Films of the Classic Era (1940–1959)*. That's right, seven-hundred-forty-five. It is no coincidence that the number of titles described as film noir has expanded with the growth of film studies. Since a finite number of movies were produced between 1940 and 1959, perhaps the archeological search for more titles is nearing an end. Of course, that range of years applies only to cycle advocates. Genre and style advocates have a virtual bottomless pit of films available to them.

Film noir, as a term, was born during the summer of 1946, when French critics reacted to what they considered a new type of Hollywood crime film. *The Maltese Falcon*; *Laura*; *Double Indemnity*; *Murder, My Sweet*; and *The Woman in the Window*, though released over three years in the United States, arrived in close proximity in Paris and formed the first wave. A few months later, *This Gun for Hire* (1942), *The Killers* (1946), *The Lady in the Lake* (1947), *Gilda* (1946), and *The Big Sleep* (1946) appeared. There was something remarkable, however difficult to define, about these films, that set them apart from other suspenseful crime melodramas. The authors of the first full-length book on film noir recognized this difference and were far more discriminating than their film studies descendants about which titles met the standard for inclusion. Raymond Borde and Etienne Chaumeton, French authors of *Panorama du Film Noir Americain* (1955), were film enthusiasts who came to their positions through extensive movie viewing. They did not create a theory, and then admit all films that met elements of that definition. Borde and Chaumeton watched numerous films from the period, and then developed an admittedly subjective sense of which films were at the center and which were at the periphery. Unfortunately, their classifications are too vague to be appropriated for this discussion.

In *Dark Cinema* (1984), Jon Tuska argues for the distinction between movies that belong to the category of film noir and others that employ the noir visual style but do not belong. According to Tuska, the difference between film noir, film *gris* (gray film), and melodrama lies in the narrative resolution (177). The melodrama is defined as a story that features a romance in the midst of other happenings and a relative happy ending concerning the couple. The difference between the film gris and the melodrama is that the romance in the melodrama leads to marriage or the suggestion of marriage, while the outcome of the romance is less certain in film gris. In film noir, the affair can hardly be called a romance, and the resolution is at least unclear, and often hostile and deadly.

Tuska argues that a film featuring a conventional romance and a happy ending undermines the bleak, pessimistic outlook associated with noir, so further designations are required. Tuska illustrates his point using three films made in 1944: *Laura, The Big Sleep*,[7] and *Double Indemnity*. In *Laura*, it is clear at the end that Laura Hunt and detective Mark McPherson will marry, it is uncertain how long the romance will last between Vivian Rutledge and Philip Marlowe in *The Big Sleep*, and the affair between Phyllis Dietrichson and Walter Neff leads to betrayal and death in *Double Indemnity*. Tuska classifies *Laura* as melodrama, *The Big Sleep* as film gris and *Double Indemnity* as film noir. Tuska provides a filmography that labels each movie, and while I disagree with him about certain films,[8] I wholeheartedly support his effort to provide much-needed restraint.

I intend to be faithful to the original impulses of Borde and Chaumeton that described film noir as a special category distinct from other melodramas and thrillers of the 1940s and 1950s.[9] Because I contend that American noir precedes the alleged introduction of existentialism from France, except for a few references to later movies, I will restrict myself to the original film noir period with one exception. Though *Chinatown* was released in 1974, the film can be seen as a commentary on films from the original period and brilliantly summarizes several important noir elements. I will follow Tuska's lead by examining the movies within the period that are most effectively noir. It is not my position that any and every movie every described as film noir qualifies as existentialist, but I submit that films most deserving of the name represent a poor man's existentialism.

ENDNOTES

1. Future quotes without page numbers were obtained from the film version.
2. Some essays by William James are notable exceptions. But James emphasizes the positive characteristics associated with existentialism, and hard-boiled fiction and film noir emphasize the negative. I will say more about these distinctions in what follows.
3. A case can be made that *Stranger on the Third Floor* (1940) is actually the first film of the cycle and *Odds Against Tomorrow* (1959) is actually the last film of the cycle.
4. The first (and for many years the only) book-length study of the films, *Panorama du Film Noir Americain*, was published by French authors Raymond Borde and Etienne Chaumeton in 1955.
5. There are very few noir titles between 1941 and 1944.
6. In 2001 the Library of America published hardcover editions (in four volumes) of Hammett's and Chandler's work.
7. *The Big Sleep* was actually filmed during 1944, but its release was delayed until 1946 so that certain scenes between Bogart and Bacall could be reshot.
8. In some cases "happy" romantic endings do not undermine the noir effect. Either the romantic subplot is overwhelmed by the atmosphere, or the ending is so unconvincingly tacked on that it can be ignored.
9. In *More than Night*, James Naremore makes a compelling case that film noir cannot be satisfactorily defined. Nevertheless, I feel compelled to offer a working definition for readers.

CHAPTER 1

THE EXISTENTIAL METAPHYSICS OF NOIR

"[A] clean orderly sane responsible affair."
—Sam Spade in Hammett's *The Maltese Falcon* (444)

In Dashiell Hammett's *The Maltese Falcon*, private eye Sam Spade relates the details of a former case to his client, Brigid O'Shaunessey, which expresses the noir detective's existential metaphysics. A real estate man named Flitcraft went to lunch one day and never returned. He disappeared, Spade says, "like a fist when you open your hand" (Hammett, *Maltese Falcon* 443). There was no reason to suspect that Flitcraft had met with foul play or had planned his disappearance. Mr. and Mrs. Flitcraft were on good terms and they had two small children. Flitcraft was worth over two hundred thousand dollars, but he could not have had more than fifty or sixty dollars in his pocket when he inexplicably vanished in 1922. Seven years later, Mrs. Flitcraft came to the detective agency in Seattle, where Spade then worked, claiming that someone had seen a man who looked like her husband in Spokane. Spade took the case and discovered that the identified man was indeed Flitcraft, who was living under the name Charles Pierce. He now ran a successful automobile business and was married (again) with a baby son. Flitcraft was not at all remorseful about what he had done, but he was concerned that he might not be able to convey the reasonableness of his actions.

Spade tells Brigid that on the way to lunch that fateful day, Flitcraft passed a construction site and a beam falling eight to ten stories smacked the pavement beside him. The beam struck close enough to Flitcraft that a piece of sidewalk chipped off and struck him in the cheek, which still bore the scar. Spade explained that Flitcraft "felt like somebody had taken the lid off life and let him look at the works" (Hammett, *Maltese Falcon* 443). Flitcraft's experience revealed what were for him the concealed forces operating the world and disclosed the underlying reality of the universe. We cannot know what Flitcraft actually *saw*, but we can draw some metaphysical conclusions from Spade's account and interpretation of Flitcraft's experience and response.

According to Spade, Flitcraft went to Seattle that very afternoon, and from there took a boat to San Francisco. After a couple of years spent wandering, Flitcraft drifted back to the Northwest, finally settling in Spokane. He soon married a woman who did not look like his first wife but who was more similar to her than dissimilar. Flitcraft's actions were reasonable to him because his brush with death jolted his sense of reality. Spade explains that Flitcraft had been a good husband, father, and citizen simply because he was most comfortable "in step with his surroundings." His behavior was consistent with his experience. Flitcraft had believed that life was "a clean orderly sane responsible affair" (444). His encounter on the way to lunch taught that he had been wrong and that the world was "fundamentally none of these things." According to Spade, Flitcraft "knew that men died haphazard like that, and lived only while blind chance spared them." Flitcraft had lived a sensible, orderly life when he believed himself "in step with his surroundings," but now that he had seen "the works" he decided to alter his life accordingly. If his life could be ended randomly by a falling beam, then he would adjust himself to the randomness of the world by randomly going away (Hammett, *Maltese Falcon* 443).

Sam Spade no doubt had numerous interesting cases to share. The narration tells us that the detective began the story without any preliminary. We should not interpret this statement to mean that Spade chose the story randomly. His interpretation of Flitcraft's actions tells us that this case is symbolic of Spade's own existential vision of the underlying reality of the world. It is Spade who asserts that Flitcraft *knew* rather than *believed* that men died haphazardly and were spared only by blind chance. Spade explains, "Flitcraft adjusted himself to beams falling, and then no more of them fell, and he adjusted himself to them not falling" (Hammett, *Maltese Falcon* 445). Once the lid on life was securely fastened again and the shock of his experience faded, Flitcraft drifted back into his former way of life, if not with his former family. Flitcraft carries the small scar on his cheek as a reminder of his experience, but the typical noir protagonist is more deeply and permanently scarred by metaphysical revelation.

The tale of Flitcraft, as told by Spade, demonstrates that awareness of metaphysical reality is obtained through personal experience, usually under extreme duress. Flitcraft, like most people, was comfortable with the notion that life in the world is "a clean orderly sane responsible affair." Recognition that the world is fundamentally none of these things is not achieved through intellectual means but is realized by way of an encounter that cannot be ignored and perhaps not expressed. As Spade tells Brigid, Flitcraft was not ashamed of his actions; he was only concerned that he might not be able to convey their reasonableness. Existential awareness is an individual attainment, and the reasons for one's actions, therefore, are difficult to articulate to others. Another man, following a near fatal accident, might have rushed home to embrace his wife and children, to cling to the most loving and stable elements in his life as a means of countering the effects of his unsettling experience. The response to such an incident will be just as contingent as the event was uncertain, for it can differ among individuals, but the disturbance it creates cannot be denied.

When Flitcraft looked at the works, he saw the *randomness of existence*. The world is not so utterly chaotic as to be incomprehensible, but it is marked by contingency—by the unforeseeable and uncontrollable. *The Asphalt Jungle* (1950), based on the W. R. Burnett novel of the same title, began a subcategory of heist noir, in which a team is carefully assembled to commit an intricately planned robbery. Though the theft in a heist noir is usually accomplished, fortuitous, and incalculable, consequences unravel its aftermath. For such schemes to succeed, everything must go according to plan. Ultimately something unexpected happens to spoil the outcome, effectively demonstrating that the world is too complex and unpredictable for such plans to achieve their objectives.

In *The Asphalt Jungle*, Irwin "Doc" Riedenschneider, recently released from prison, masterminds the robbery of more than $1 million in gems from Belletier's, a swanky jewelry store. The plan calls for the group to enter the store from underground where they will first disable the alarm. Once inside, they will elude the security beam near the vault. Louie Ciavelli will confirm his claim that he can open any safe in four minutes or less. They will grab the merchandise and retrace their steps back to where Gus Minissi will be waiting with the getaway car. Alonzo Emmerich, a successful criminal attorney, has arranged to fence the goods through respectable business contacts. Doc and Dix Handley will rendezvous with Emmerich immediately after the robbery to exchange the jewels for cash.

Riedenschneider spent his prison term refining his perfect plan, considering all potential problems but learns that even a criminal mastermind is powerless against a contingent world in which almost anything can happen. "Put in hours and hours of planning to get everything down to the last detail. Then what?" He asks, "Burglar alarms start going off all over the place for no sensible reason. A gun fires of its own accord and a man is shot. A broken down old harness bull not good for anything but chasing kids has to trip over us. What can you do against blind accidents?" Bad luck can defeat even the most meticulously planned affair. The crew disables the burglar alarm, but the explosion that opens the safe triggers alarms in adjacent buildings, drawing the police. As they make their exit, a security guard happens by. Dix slugs the guard causing him to drop his weapon, but the gun strikes the floor and accidentally discharges a bullet that catches Louie in the belly. By the end of the film, all members of the gang are caught or killed through a series of seemingly random occurrences.

In existential hard-boiled fiction and film noir, the experience of the contingency of existence is often accompanied by or challenged by the feeling that outcomes are determined. Flitcraft went to lunch, as he had countless times without incident, but that particular day, a beam happened to fall a few feet away and his life was altered.

In *I Married a Dead Man* (1948), authored by Cornell Woolrich, the narration presents the positions of the advocates for chance and fate. A young woman traveling by train, exhausted and unable to find a seat, sits on her suitcase near a young couple. Helen Georgesson's life will undergo considerable change because of her location. Pregnant, deserted, and without family or funds, Helen is befriended by a young, recently married woman, Patrice, who is also pregnant but traveling with her husband, Hugh. There is a train wreck and Helen awakens in the hospital to find herself mistaken for Patrice.[1] Hugh's affluent parents have never met or seen Patrice, and have made preparations to take care of their deceased son's wife and their grandchild. For the sake of her baby, Helen decides to accept the mistaken identity. After a short period of relative tranquility, much trouble follows.

As Helen comes to rest on her suitcase the narrator asks, "What makes you stop, when you have stopped, just where you have stopped? What is it, what? Is it something, or is it nothing? Why not a yard short, why not a yard more? Why just there where you are, and nowhere else?" (Woolrich 810). The alternative explanations offered are chance and fate:

> Some say: It's just blind chance, and if you hadn't stopped there, you would have stopped at the next place. Your story would have been different then. You weave your own story as you go along.

> But others say: You could not have stopped any place else but this even if you had wanted to. It was decreed, it was ordered, you

> were meant to stop at this spot and no other. Your story is there
> waiting for you, it has been waiting for you there a hundred years,
> long before you were born, and you cannot change a comma of
> it. Everything you do, you have to do. You are the twig, and the
> water you float on swept you here. You are the leaf and the breeze
> you were borne on blew you here. This is your story, and you
> cannot escape it; you are only the player, not the stage manager
> (Woolrich 810).

Flitcraft's experience, as interpreted by Sam Spade, offers the same problem of interpretation, though it initially appears as a blind chance encounter. He went to lunch that day as he had countless other times, but at that particular time, a falling beam *just happened* to land a few feet away. Had he been positioned a few feet in one direction, perhaps he would have been killed—a few yards away and perhaps the falling beam would have had little significance. The position that your story is waiting for you, determined to occur, is expressed by *Detour*'s Al Roberts, who says, "[F]ate or some mysterious force can put the finger on you or me for no good reason at all." One view describes the accidental, the feeling that fortuity is responsible. The alternative view emphasizes causal determination, as though events follow from necessity. Existential awareness in film noir begins with recognition of randomness as the underlying reality of the world, but most noir protagonists express an attitude similar to Robert's, that fate is the responsible force. Certain noir films, such as *Detour* and *Criss Cross* are fascinating because they combine these seemingly conflicting viewpoints into a single experience.

In *Detour* (1945), piano player Al Roberts encounters an incredible series of circumstances while hitchhiking from New York to Los Angeles to reunite with his singer girlfriend, Sue. Long after Roberts has ceased counting the days and weeks of his journey, he is no further than Arizona. Roberts receives a lift from Charles Haskell, who tells him, "You're in luck this time. I'm going all the way." Haskell explains the noticeably severe scratches on the back of his hand, telling Roberts that he tangled with the most vicious animal there is: a woman. Roberts takes his turn driving while Haskell sleeps and after several miles it begins to rain. He cannot wake Haskell, so he stops to put up the roof on the convertible. Haskell still will not budge, so Roberts opens the passenger door. Haskell's body tumbles out and his head strikes a rock. Haskell is dead, though it is not clear whether he was dead before the blow. Certain he would not be believed if he told the truth, Roberts decides the only alternative is to hide the corpse and exchange identities with the dead man. The next day, Roberts offers a ride to a hitchhiking woman named Vera, who after a few miles asks, "What did you do with the body?" Vera was Haskell's earlier passenger and recognizes the car and Haskell's clothes on Roberts. Vera uses her leverage to force Roberts to drive to Los Angeles, sell the vehicle, and give her the money, until she learns from the newspaper that Haskell, who ran away as a boy, is heir to a fortune. Vera insists that Roberts impersonate Haskell to collect the inheritance. Late one night, in their hotel room, an angry and intoxicated Vera threatens to expose Roberts. She grabs the telephone and rushes into the bedroom, locking the door. Panic-stricken, Roberts yanks the cord, not realizing that the drunken Vera has carelessly wrapped it around her neck. He kicks open the door to find Vera on the bed, strangled. Roberts abandons his plans to join Sue and hitchhikes aimlessly, ever fearful that his next ride will be in a police car.

One aspect of contingency is coincidence, in which a series of accidental events seem planned or arranged. The coincidences involved in Robert's experience lend themselves to the blind chance interpretation but also to the sense that some manipulative power is at work. As he begins his flashback narration, Roberts tells us that hitchhiking is dangerous because "you never know what's in store for you." What were the odds that the driver who offered him a ride would suddenly die, either from some unknown ailment or by freak accident? What were the odds that Roberts would offer a lift to the very same woman who earlier rode with Haskell? What were the odds that the telephone cord would be around Vera's neck to strangle her as Roberts yanked the cord? The odds against these coincidences are so staggering that, at the end of his ordeal, Roberts concludes that some malevolent force was out to get him.

Coincidence has fatal effects for Steve Thompson in *Criss Cross* (1949), who has recently returned to Los Angeles and become reacquainted with his troublesome ex-wife, Anna. When she fails to appear for a date, Thompson learns that Anna went to Reno to marry Slim Dundee, a local gangster. Anna claims she turned to the pursuing Dundee after she was warned to keep away from Steve by police Lt. Ramirez, at the behest of Steve's mother. Steve and the unhappy Anna want to run away together, but they need money. Thompson volunteers to be the inside man in a robbery of the armored car company where he works and joins forces with Dundee, but he stipulates that the elderly driver, Pops, is not to be harmed. During the robbery Dundee shoots Pops, Thompson wounds Dundee, and Thompson is himself wounded by another member of the gang. The hospitalized Thompson is considered a hero for saving half the payroll, but his friend, Ramirez, suspects that Thompson was involved in the robbery. An agent of Dundee, posing as a visitor, forces Thompson out of the hospital at gunpoint, but Thompson bribes him to drive to his rendezvous with Anna. When Thompson arrives, Anna is preparing to leave without him. Before they can depart, separately or together, the crippled Dundee arrives and kills them both.

Thompson's voiceover narration begins as he is driving to the robbery. As he reflects, he is not sure how to describe the forces responsible for his condition, though he is certain those forces are metaphysical. His voiceover tells us that when he returned to Los Angeles, he intended to stay away from Anna, but "from the start, it all went one way. It was in the cards, or fate, or a jinx, or whatever you want to call it. But right from the start," Thompson walks from the streetcar to his mother's home, but when he arrives, no one is there, and he cannot get in.

Thompson's words express that the path was intended for him, as one of Woolrich's possibilities suggests:

> I went down to the drugstore to call Ramirez, Pete Ramirez. We grew up together. He was an old friend. I thought I might drop over and kill and hour. But it all went one way that sunny afternoon. It was in the cards. His wife told me he was away somewhere working on a case. Pete always had the night shift, but this

afternoon he was on duty. This particular afternoon. And then somehow there I was in the Roundup. The old place. The old hangout. There I was looking for her.

Thompson shares his awareness of the coincidences involved in the circumstances that lead to his destruction. What if he had not returned home that particular day at that particular time? What if he had not been locked out? What if Pete Ramirez had been home as he usually was instead of out on a case? What if he had not happened to go to the old hangout, the Roundup?

Coincidence combines the experience of the accidental with the experience of contrived circumstances, which contributes to the feeling that some metaphysical force has engineered the outcome. As Yogi Berra allegedly put it, "It's too coincidental to be a coincidence." Though the narrator in *I Married a Dead Man* presents the blind chance and determinism positions as though they are in conflict, the narration does not explicitly develop this tension further. In fact, for noir characters, these positions are usually not in conflict. Virtually all noir protagonists, initially or belatedly, recognize contingency as the underlying reality of the world. This acceptance characterizes their status as noir protagonists. The attitude concerning fate is always expressed (when it is expressed) retrospectively. Al Roberts does not begin his cross-country journey believing that some mysterious force is out to get him, but he offers this explanation in flashback narration when incredible coincidence strikes not once, but twice. Steve Thompson reflects that his condition was "in the cards, or fate, or a jinx" only after looking back at a string of coincidences that lands him among professional criminals executing a robbery. Noir characters acknowledge the randomness of existence; the issue of fate is raised as they desperately try to comprehend how so much bad luck, in the form of coincidences, could befall them.

The acceptance of contingency and the explanation of fate are best understood when one appreciates the noir protagonist's response to the underlying reality of the world. The metaphysical characteristics of contingency contradict the notion that life is "a clean orderly sane responsible affair," and instead assert that life is a gamble and gambling is a way of life. Noir protagonists are often given little choice but to gamble, as was the case with Al Roberts. Once Haskell collapsed, Roberts could only play the cards he was dealt. The gamble is usually a losing proposition, but the noir gambler, forced to play under adverse circumstances, is even more likely than usual to fail. The explanation of fate is subsequently offered as a soothing application over wounds that never heal. Such rationalization is needed in a world that makes gambling against long odds necessary. The existential metaphysics of noir establishes the conditions that make gambling unavoidable, whether or not the protagonist's gamble is voluntary or compelled.

Jeff Bailey and Kathie Moffett are at a roulette table in *Out of the Past* (1947). Kathie places a large sum on a single number and Jeff warns her, "That's no way to win." She asks, "Is there a way to win?" After briefly considering the question, Jeff replies, "There's a way to lose more slowly." Their exchange expresses the inevitability of defeat that is prevalent in film noir, where the gamble frequently involves one's very life. Bailey's remark indicates that the only real decision is about how one chooses to lose. Some gamblers insert small change into casino slot machines, expanding the time their money will last, increasing the number of times they can play. Most noir characters liken that approach to slow death and take the high-risk alternative, though they accelerate the danger. In some cases, members of the latter group are forced by circumstances to take such chances, but sometimes they consciously decide to risk it all in one expensive roll of the dice.

Those familiar with the casino business know there is no shortage of gamblers who believe they have a system that will enable them to beat the house. In the film noir masterpiece *Double Indemnity* (1944), insurance salesman Walter Neff expresses the belief that his professional expertise increases the odds in his favor. Neff teams with his newfound lover, Phyllis Dietrichson, as they develop and implement a scheme to kill her husband and collect the insurance money. Neff's voiceover explains why he thinks he will succeed: "You're like the guy behind the roulette wheel," he says, "watching the customers to make sure they don't crook the house. And then one night, you get to thinking how you could crook the house yourself, and do it smart, because you've got that wheel right under your hands. And you know every notch in it by heart."

Neff's experience is especially valuable for this discussion because his plan to beat the odds involves an accident policy. The accident is another aspect of contingency prevalent in the noir world. In *The Asphalt Jungle*, criminal mastermind Doc Riedenschneider exclaimed his impotence against what he termed "blind accidents." In *Double Indemnity*, Neff intends to succeed where Riedenschneider fails, and he challenges the metaphysical reality of the noir world by attempting to make a mockery of the randomness of existence.

Neff intends to make it appear that Mr. Dietrichson[2] was accidentally killed by a fall from a moving train. Insurance companies offer double indemnity clauses, which pay twice the face value of the policy for such rare accidents. Dietrichson is not interested in accident insurance, but Neff cleverly includes the paperwork with the auto renewal forms. Dietrichson is scheduled to travel to Palo Alto for a college reunion. He usually drives, but he will have to be convinced to journey by train. Neff intends to kill Dietrichson on the way to the station, impersonate him on the train, then proceed to the observation car and jump off unobserved. Phyllis will be waiting at a prearranged location, and they will dump Dietrichson's dead body on the tracks.

Neff intends to fabricate an accident; that is, he will try to create an unexpected event. But before Neff can implement his plan, a genuine accident occurs: Dietrichson suffers a broken leg. This chance occurrence appears as good fortune for Neff, for Dietrichson cannot drive and will have to take the train. However, Neff does not treat the happening as an *accident*, but as an *incident* to incorporate into his plan. Neff does not resemble Dietrichson, but the conspicuous leg cast and crutches should divert attention away from Neff's face, which is obscured by a hat during the impersonation. In his eagerness to execute his scheme and manufacture his own accident, Neff fails to treat Dietrichson's incident as a genuine accident and leaves himself vulnerable to the revenge of the metaphysical god of accidents.

Every detail of the plan is flawlessly executed. Neff is crouched behind the back seat as Phyllis drives her husband to the train station. When she signals that the coast is clear, Neff strangles Dietrichson, and he and Phyllis complete their work. Neff phoned a coworker to establish an alibi for the evening and told the garage attendant that he would not need his car. He slipped in and out of his apartment unseen and rigged his telephone and doorbell so he would know if anyone called or stopped by. Neff walked from his apartment to Dietrichson's house, and after the murder, Phyllis dropped him off blocks away from his address. The only thing left to do is go out for a meal, passing the garage attendant, to confirm that he has been in all evening.

Though Neff is confident about his achievement, on his way to the drugstore his voiceover reports the feeling of doom:

> That was all there was to it. Nothing had slipped, nothing had been over-looked; there was nothing to give us away. And yet, Keyes, as I was walking down the street to the drugstore, suddenly it came to me that everything would go wrong. It sounds crazy, Keyes, but it's true, so help me: I couldn't hear my own footsteps. It was the walk of a dead man.

Neff expresses the retrospective attitude common to gambling noir protagonists and identifies fate as his enemy, but as usual, the adversary is also the randomness of existence. Neff seems aware that he cannot beat the house, though he is not certain how he will be defeated. He is ultimately undone by the genuine accident and by the accident he manufactures.

Neff's superior and friend, Barton Keyes, is the company's meticulous claims investigator. His "little man" (his gut) tells him which claims are phony, and the Dietrichson case gives him indigestion. Unlike Neff, Keyes treats Dietrichson's broken leg as a legitimate accident, which it is, and asks the pertinent question, which Neff did not. Dietrichson obtained accident insurance, and then broke his leg. He had an accident. Why didn't he file a claim? Keyes considers the possibility that Dietrichson did not know he had insurance but dismisses that idea because the trusted Neff administered the policy. Nevertheless, Keyes' curiosity is peaked, and he is a relentless inspector. As an experienced insurance salesman, Neff should have anticipated this problem. He carefully accounted for every aspect of the murder, but because he did not treat Dietrichson's incident as an accident, but accounted for it as part of the planned murder, he disregarded the accident's consequences.

Dietrichson's legitimate accident is examined due to the absence of a claim; Neff's fabricated accident is inspected because a claim is anticipated by the insurance company. Norton, a dim-witted executive, attempts to reach a settlement with Phyllis, telling her that the company suspects her husband's death was suicide. This conclusion would eliminate the company's liability, but after Phyllis departs, Keyes explains that suicide cannot be defended. The actuary table includes every incident of suicide, and there is not a single recorded case of death by a fall from moving train. Besides, at the train's rate of speed, no man could jump off with the expectation that the fall would kill him. Keyes' explanation pertains to accidental death as well, and he expresses how absurd Neff's incident appears when it is examined as an accident:

> Look. A man takes out an accident policy that is worth a hundred thousand dollars if he is killed on a train. Then, two weeks later, he *is* killed on a train. And not in a train accident, mind you, but falling off some silly observation car. Do you know what the mathematical probability of that is, Walter? One out of I don't know how many billions. And add to that the broken leg. It just can't be the way it looks, Walter. Something has been worked on us.

Keyes' analysis identifies a problem with Neff's plan to make Dietrichson's death appear as an accident. An accident is an unexpected chance event, but Neff wants two certain outcomes, which means he must eliminate chance from the operation. Neff wants Dietrichson dead, but chance can only provide probability of death, not certainty, so Neff kills Dietrichson before they reach the station to ensure the outcome. Neff also wants to survive the fall, which is supposed to have killed Dietrichson, so his jump and Dietrichson's manufactured fall occurs soon after the train departs from the station. Were Neff to jump from the train once it reaches its regular rate of speed, he risks injury or being killed. By eliminating the possibility of such an accident, Neff also removes the quality of chance that defines accidents. Neff could have jumped from where he did and placed Dietrichson's body near the tracks at a point where the train would have reached its maximum speed. Such foresight would have required Neff to treat his incident as a genuine accident, but his chosen approach involves disregard for the underlying metaphysical reality of the noir world. Neff, the gambler, is not interested in cooperating with contingency but wishes to "crook the house" by cheating chance itself.

Once suicide and accident are ruled out by Keyes' examination, only murder remains as a possibility. Because the fall could not have killed Dietrichson, Keyes reasons that the victim must have been murdered and then placed on the tracks, which also means the man who boarded the train was an imposter. Phyllis, as the beneficiary, is the prime suspect, and she evidently has a male accomplice.

Neff is finished manufacturing accidents, but when he warns Phyllis that they must abort their plan to collect the insurance money, he is confronted with contingency in the form of the unforeseen and uncontrollable. He agrees with Phyllis that she will arouse suspicion if she does not sue but says they will have to take that *chance*. If the case comes to court, certain incriminating evidence will undoubtedly surface concerning Phyllis' proximity to the death of the previous Mrs. Dietrichson. Phyllis was seen modeling a black hat and veil a few days before her husband died. Because this information could only have come from Lola Dietrichson, her adversarial step-daughter, Phyllis accuses Neff of cheating on her with Lola. Neff admits spending time with Lola to keep her quiet, but Phyllis becomes the irrational scorned woman and confirms her determination to sue the insurance company even if it means the gas chamber for both of them.

Walter Neff is the definitive noir gambler. He is *wised-up* enough to know he cannot win, but places the ultimate wager nonetheless. Since the randomness of existence is the key metaphysical property of the noir world, Neff cannot transform randomness into order and cheat chance. He initially tells Phyllis that no plan involving murder and an insurance company can possibly succeed. "They'll hang you as sure as ten dimes will buy a dollar," Neff remarks. His voiceover narration explains that he murdered Dietrichson for money and a woman, acknowledging the irony that he did not acquire either, but subsequent comments reveal that the thrill of the gamble was his greater motivation. Neff is too smart for his dull job peddling insurance to suckers who are, in effect, wagering against themselves, so he spends his time daydreaming about beating the system. He explains that Phyllis provided "the shill to put down the bet" in his plan to "crook the house." Neff does not gamble against prohibitive odds because he truly believes he can win. He risks his life because the alternative is a boring, meaningless existence. The only time he seems excited about living is during the planning and execution of the murder. The randomness of existence, though fatal, provides an exciting ride for the intrepid gambler with nothing to lose.

Horace McCoy's 1934 novel, *They Shoot Horses Don't They?*, sets his protagonists at a Great Depression-era marathon dance, to demonstrate the sense of entrapment in meaningless activity that leads to indifference to living. Robert and Gloria feel forced to enter the contest because they are impoverished, unemployed, and desperate. Contestants receive food and shelter while they participate, and the couple hopes to win the $1,000 prize. The marathon dance is a gamble, for contestants are competing against long odds. The contest offers Robert and Gloria the ability to lose more slowly. The marathon structure also allows McCoy to offer an existential experience of time and space.

The meaninglessness of activity is established by the rules and events of the marathon dance. The contest is called a *dance*, but contestants are not actually required to dance, they must merely keep moving enough to avoid being disqualified. Most of the time, contestants sway minimally, occasionally shifting their feet or changing direction to create the impression of greater movement. Gloria describes the marathon dance as a merry-go-round, capturing the experience of going in circles to no particular purpose and growing dizzy in the process. In order to reinforce the effect, each day's events include a derby, in which contestants are required to race in a circle around the dance floor for fifteen minutes. This is a grueling competition between couples, but there is no prize for winning a derby, confirming its purposelessness.

The marathon dance is actually a war of attrition. The rules are arranged less to determine a victor than to eliminate the weak. The couple that finishes last in a derby is disqualified from the contest. Nurses are stationed in the pit during derbies so that when contestants collapse, as contest managers anticipate they will, they can receive medical attention. Partners are required to run extra laps to make up for these absences, increasing their chances of tiring. Activities like derbies and sprints (the latter are two-minute, high intensity drills), are presented for the amusement of the spectators, who would probably not pay to watch couples sway about indefinitely. The primary objective for the contestants, other than food and shelter, is to avoid disqualification and remain gamblers in meaningless activity.

The marathon dance is the last alternative for Robert and Gloria as they perceive it. They are struggling actors unable to find even bit parts as extras, and they cannot find any other work, either. Robert's last job was temporary, substituting for a friend. Gloria stole to get herself arrested, but the detectives felt sorry for her and released her. There is no place for them to turn outside the contest. Robert opens the door to the dance hall and describes what he sees as the end of the world. The realm beyond the marathon dance, for all intents and purposes, no longer has meaning for them. Their existence is confined to a space thirty feet wide and two hundred feet long. This perception is reinforced by rules that prohibit contestants to leave the building or approach the exits. Spectators are able to come and go as they please, but contestants are trapped inside by circumstances, desperation, and contest rules.

The couples are disconnected from nature as though they were locked in a penitentiary. Robert is able to expand his space only for a few minutes per day by moving toward the platform at just the right time. Robert shares,

> It was nice down there about this time of the afternoon. There was a big triangle of sunshine that came through the double window above the bar in the Palm Garden. It only lasted about ten minutes but during those ten minutes I moved slowly about in it (I had to move to keep from being disqualified) letting it cover me completely. It was the first time I had ever appreciated the sun. I watched the triangle on the floor get smaller and smaller. Finally it closed altogether and started up my legs. It crawled up my body like a living thing. When it got to my chin I stood on my toes, to keep my head in it as long as possible. I did not close my eyes. I kept them wide open, looking straight into the sun. It did not blind me at all. In a moment it was gone. (McCoy 135)

Robert's expression is like that of a convict who receives sunlight through a crevice in his cell for a few minutes each day, with only that time to commune with nature and feel like a human being.

During the marathon dance, time is carefully regimented, monitored, documented, and announced. The schedule consists of one hour and fifty minutes of *dancing* followed by a ten-minute rest period. Sprints are exactly two minutes long; derbies are precisely fifteen minutes in duration. Frequent updates of elapsed hours are posted and announced. Meanwhile, the contestants experience time in a manner that is less linear than existential.

Two minutes of time objectively quantified always measures two minutes. The amount of time elapsed in two minutes subjectively measured depends upon the experience of the human being living through that time. Two minutes spent having a tooth drilled without anesthesia can seem like an eternity. The *same* two minutes spent resting before the dentist resumes drilling seems to pass in an instant. The dentist and the patient are likely to have very different subjective experiences of that time, though the objective measurements are equal.[3]

In *They Shoot Horses Don't They?*, the perception of how time is appreciated differs between those who run the contest and those who perform in it. The ten-minute intervals in which contestants are freed from the requirement to dance are referred to as *rest* periods by contest officials. Robert explains that these times are better used "learning to eat your sandwich while you shaved, learning to eat when you went to the john, when you had your feet fixed" (McCoy 118). The ten minutes each day that Robert spends with his ray of light is more of a rest period, though he is required to be active.

Rocky, an emcee, never tires of announcing to spectators that after so many hundred hours, the dancers are still fresh. Why would he tire? Rocky has not been on his feet for more than the equivalent of a month, as these contestants have. He is fond of calling for sprints during the final two minutes of dance periods, also for the benefit of relaxing spectators, while contestants study the second hand of the clock, desperately anticipating temporary relief. Rocky always refers to the two-minute interval as a *little* sprint; only two short minutes remain until the rest period begins. Those same two minutes are spent in agony by Gloria, who says, "God, the hand on the clock moves slow" (McCoy 119).

Baseball has been referred to as the timeless game because it is the only major sport that is not controlled by a clock. The game does not end when the clock expires but continues until each team has had its innings. The marathon dance is not controlled by a clock either but continues until the players expire. The objective of the marathon dance is to use minutes and hours to defeat the contestants; the clock measures the effects. The teams are not actually competing against each other but against time. Human beings have limited endurance; the clock never stops. Time is organized into intervals and activities meant to exhaust the participants to the extent that they are eventually unable to continue. The extended dance periods are meant to wear away at them slowly. The quicker-paced sprints and derbies are intended to sap their strength, which in turn reduces their stamina for the longer dance sessions. The dance periods reduce their energy for the up-tempo sprints and derbies. What we have then is the merry-go-round effect that Gloria described: meaningless activity that crushes the will to persist.

Gloria is ultimately destroyed by time. She had convinced the reluctant Robert to join the marathon dance. Though already desperate and depressed, Gloria considered the contest an opportunity for survival. Eventually, the marathon dance absorbs her will to live. The relentless pounding of the second hand of the clock penetrates Gloria's fragile psyche like water dropping on a rock, inevitably wearing away her resistance until she finally cracks. The marathon dance ends prematurely due to an eruption of violence, but the pounding will not stop. Unwilling to continue dying slowly, Gloria persuades Robert to shoot her in the head because under these conditions, it is the humane thing to do. "It's the only way to get me out of my misery," she concludes (McCoy 210). After all, they shoot horses, don't they?

Time and space act as conditions of entrapment in Kenneth Fearing's 1947 novel, *The Big Clock* (filmed in 1948). George Stroud is chief editor of *Crimeways* magazine, a periodical known for locating fugitive criminals before the police and then publishing their sensational exploits. Stroud is forced to use his skills and the considerable resources of the magazine to build a trap intended to ensnare none other than himself.

Though he is an executive, Stroud immediately expresses a working man's sentiment when he tells us that the "awfulness of Monday morning is the world's great common denominator" (Fearing 444). Managers may receive more money than their poorer relations, but their sufferings are more expensive because they spend their working lives conforming to "a sort of overgrown, aimless, haphazard stenciling apparatus that kept them running to psychoanalysis, sent them to insane asylums, gave them high blood pressure, stomach ulcers, killed them off with cerebral hemorrhages and heart failure, sometimes suicide" (Fearing 468). Stroud seeks compensation in occasional extramarital affairs and is currently achieving the ultimate working man's revenge: He is having an affair with his boss' mistress, Pauline Delos.

When publishing tycoon Earl Janoth learns that Pauline has been unfaithful, he kills her during a violent argument. Janoth does not know the identity of Pauline's lover, but he learned from her where the couple spent the weekend. Janoth decides to use the resources of *Crimeways* to find Pauline's lover and frame him for the killing, and Stroud is coincidentally assigned to find the mystery man. Essentially, Stroud is looking for himself, though he is not the murderer. Stroud cannot reveal his knowledge of Janoth's guilt without incriminating himself, so he is forced to conduct the investigation as he simultaneously looks for evidence against Janoth.

Little by little, the walls close in around Stroud. He did not use his real name at his weekend stops with Pauline, but witnesses provide physical descriptions, and soon a composite of the quarry is constructed. The witness from the hotel enters Janoth Publications and happens to recognize the fugitive getting onto an elevator. Now the investigative team knows that their prey is somewhere in the building. All exits except one are sealed, and no one is allowed to leave without passing the witness at the front doors. Soon other witnesses are gathered to expand the building search, and Stroud must avoid them while spearheading the investigation. Security forces accompany the witnesses as they inspect every floor and every room. Stroud knows where the groups are searching and is able to be elsewhere, but it is only a matter of time until he is cornered and the witnesses identify him. There are only so many floors and so many rooms, and they are being eliminated one by one. Stroud is running out of space.

In the following description, Stroud's narration describes how the big clock conflates time and space, creating the effect of a rat caught in a maze:

> One runs like a mouse up the old, slow pendulum of the big clock, time, scurries around and across its huge hands, strays inside through the intricate wheels and balances and springs of the inner mechanisms, searching among the cobwebbed mazes of this machine with all its false exists and dangerous blind alleys and steep runways, natural traps and artificial baits, hunting for the true opening and the real prize. Then the clock strikes one and it is time to go, to run down the pendulum, to become again a prisoner making once more the same escape. (Fearing 393)

This rumination is delivered long before Stroud is running for his life but foreshadows that time and space, which are already present as forces of confusion and disorientation, will intensify as forces of destruction.

Early in the investigation, Stroud attempts to convince himself that he can somehow outsmart the big clock. "I could beat the machines," he ponders, "The super-clock would go on forever, it was too massive to be stopped. But it had no brains, and I did. I could escape from it" (Fearing 468). As the spatial lines of the investigation converge, Stroud realizes he has also underestimated time's awesome capacity:

> I told myself it was just a tool, a vast machine, and the machine was blind. But I had not realized its crushing power. That was insane. The machine cannot be challenged. It both creates and blots out, doing each with glacial impersonality. It measures people in the same way that is measures money, and the growth of trees, the life-span of mosquitoes and morals, the advance of time. And when the hour strikes, on the big clock, that is indeed the hour, the day, the correct time. When it says a man is right, he is right, and when it finds him wrong, he is through, with no appeal. It is as deaf as it is blind. (Fearing 493)

Time overcomes all obstacles. Stroud initially made the mistake of treating the big clock as a physical object objectively measured rather than as a metaphysical presence subjectively experienced.

The Big Clock is one of the few genuine noir stories in which coincidence and the unexpected eventually work in favor of the seemingly doomed protagonist, though only after some harrowing hours. Stroud and Pauline Delos stopped at an art gallery during their weekend affair. Stroud has a fondness for the work of an obscure painter named Louise Patterson. He and another customer became involved in a bidding contest for a painting by the artist. The mystery man's competitor, *Crimeways* investigators learn, was none other than the wildly eccentric Patterson herself. She is lured to the Janoth building by the promise of one hundred dollars to create a sketch of the phantom. Stroud, in hiding somewhere when the call is made to her, is not aware that Patterson is coming to see him. It appears that time and space have expired for Stroud. Patterson arrives and immediately recognizes Stroud as "the murderer," but she whimsically decides not to incriminate one of the few collectors of her work.

Time had not come for Stroud, but for Janoth. Earl Janoth was living on borrowed time, and his time expired. The stockholders had for some time been unhappy with profits under his leadership. Janoth is forced out of the enterprise that bears his name and commits suicide. Time made the murder investigation irrelevant. With Janoth dead, the search stops dead in its tracks. But Stroud can take little comfort in his narrow escape. There is always reason to worry because time is irresistible and relentless, as Stroud explains,

> The big clock ran everywhere, overlooked no one, omitted no one, forgot nothing, remembered nothing, knew nothing. Was nothing, I would have liked to add, but I knew better. It was just about everything. Everything there is. (Fearing 513)

No one knows where or when the noir clock will strike. Certain philosophical arguments claim that time is unreal, but now that Stroud has learned to treat time as a subjective experience, he knows better than to call it nothing.

The metaphysical themes of randomness, coincidence, the big gamble, and time and space, collide in *Brute Force* (1947), one of the most cynical and violent films of the cycle. Prison noir is made to order for matters pertaining to time and space because prisoners are confined to cells, and sentences are meted out in specific duration. Prisoners commonly refer to incarceration as "serving time." A convict may experience time in years, months, days, or hours, whichever seems least painful or more tortuous, depending on his term, crime, and disposition. Some inmates may attempt to ignore time to avoid counting the seemingly infinite number of points on the line to freedom. Prisoners serving life sentences may endure time as something that stands still or no longer matters.

The themes of time and space are introduced early in *Brute Force*. Inmate Joe Collins visits Dr. Walter's office and asks the time, and the doctor replies that it is approximately 10:30. Collins wants the exact time, and Walters checks his watch and says the time is exactly 10:27. The scene shifts to the metal workshop where the clock reads 10:27. Two inmates carrying clipboards are circulating among the convicts. At each stop, they whisper "Wilson, 10:30." At exactly 10:30, one group of prisoners stages a fight at the water cooler drawing the guards away from their stations. Meanwhile, another group of convicts carrying blowtorches converges on the aforementioned Wilson, driving him into a huge punch press. The scene shifts back to Dr. Walter's office. After the doctor receives a call about the incident, the following exchange takes place.

> WALTERS: Well this is one rap they can't hang on you, Collins. I'm your witness. Important thing, witnesses. It's lucky you asked me before exactly what time it was.
> COLLINS: Yeah, wasn't it?
> WALTERS: Fella named Wilson.
> COLLINS: Tough break. Accident?
> WALTERS: Positively. Witnesses.

Though Collins ordered Wilson's execution, a successfully manufactured accident, he cannot be accused of this killing because time and space, as much as Walters, are his alibis. Collins was not in the space of the workshop at the designated time. The witnesses to the accident were present in the applicable time and space, and their testimony cannot be challenged.

Space is described in another early scene in which inmate Spencer fondly recalls an evening in his past when he was conned out of his money and automobile by a female companion. Coy, the newest of the cellmates, asks why anyone would want to remember a story like that. Spencer replies that such an incident is worthy of reminiscence simply because it happened "on the outside." By reliving incidents from the outside, inmates temporarily expand or relocate the space of their existence. Coy asks about the strange relationship his cellmates seem to have with a poster of a woman they refer to as "Lady." "It's enough to give you the creeps," Coy says. The men explain that the portrait is the imaginative representative of their actual women. "She gets you thinking about the one you want to be with," Freshman clarifies. Though their women are in another space, on the outside, the convicts are able to bring some of that outside space inside.

Wakefield Penitentiary acts as a pressure cooker that compresses existential time and space. Walters calls the institution a "human bomb" that is always on the verge of exploding. The narrative of *Brute Force* focuses on the six inmates of cell R17, who are driven by extreme circumstances to gamble their lives in an impossible jailbreak attempt. A series of flashbacks depicts how three of the prisoners came to be incarcerated and why each is desperate to escape.

Joe Collins, the leader, is seen visiting the girlfriend he first met on a chance stop when his car ran out of gas. Ruth has cancer and is confined to a wheelchair. She needs money for an operation, and Collins hoped his take of the robbery would finance her surgery. The prisoner known as Soldier is shown married to an Italian woman named Gina during the war. He brings her food when he is able, but his prohibited visit is interrupted by the chance arrival of an Army patrol. When one of her comrades attempts to expose Soldier, Gina shoots him, and Soldier takes the blame. Inmate Lister embezzled funds from his company to buy a fur coat for his wife, Cora. As he presents the gift his wife adores because owning it makes her feel "like somebody," he explains that he was fearful that they were headed for a breakup, for she wanted things, and he was always strapped for money. *Brute Force* portrays the inmates of cell R17 as honorable working-class men pressured by economic circumstances to commit crimes. These men had the bad luck to get caught, but considering the risks they took, they were likely to get caught. The film suggests that these men received a *raw deal*[4] from life and are paying the price for not having enough money to make their problems go away. They still experience pressure from outside space, which sometimes painfully penetrates their inside space, and from time, the inmates' most brutal enemy. Collins' girlfriend, Ruth, will not undergo surgery unless Joe is by her side. Ruth does not know Collins is in prison, and he will not allow her to be told. Time is a factor in treating her cancer. Soldier only hopes he can somehow find Gina, if he ever gets back to Italy. Time has moved her farther away. Lister was fearful of losing Cora when he was a free man. His concern is aggravated by his lengthy prison sentence.

Time has further separated them. Each convict feels an urgent need to escape *now*.

The coordination of time and space are essential aspects of their escape plan. Collins learns from an old, dying convict (who is running out of time) that the guard tower is vulnerable to attack. Collins is sent back to Soldier, whose combat experience provides the key. The guard tower has only one machine gun mount, which means it can only defend one side of its structure at a time. If two groups of prisoners can launch attacks from inside and outside the prison, one group may be able to seize the tower and throw the lever that opens the massive doors to the penitentiary. The plan requires attacks from two spaces, inside and outside the prison, and they must be synchronized.

The problem of getting outside the prison is solved when the inmates of R17 are unexpectedly assigned to work in the drainpipe as punishment. The drainpipe, located just outside prison walls, occupies mysterious space for the convicts because none of them know where the drainpipe begins or where it will end. The space inside the drainpipe is so filthy that it has claimed the lives of several inmates, so space brought time to an end for those men. This hazardous duty ironically appears as a stroke of luck for the crew, for it provides the opportunity for an outside assault.

Time is critical for this escape because the attacks must be simultaneous. Collins joins forces with a senior prisoner named Gallagher,[5] whose men will launch the inside attack while Collins' men strike from outside. Time also involves planning time and determining the optimum time to be in the proper spaces. Gallagher is shocked to learn that Collins intends to go tomorrow afternoon. "This kind of thing takes planning," Gallagher insists. But Collins vehemently disagrees. Gallagher views time as opportunity for planning and organization; the more time the better. Collins views time as the enemy. Over Gallagher's objections that they should wait, Collins snaps "No! The longer you wait the longer the odds. The first guy stalls. A second gets cold feet. A third guy can't keep his mouth shut." Collins believes he is improving the odds by moving quickly. Moving quickly means less time for something to go wrong.

Collins' concern demonstrates the extent of their gamble. Everything must go according to plan if they are to have any chance to succeed, and Collins hopes to reduce the opportunity for mistakes. Collins is most worried about human weakness, as the aforementioned statement indicates. In the noir world, metaphysical forces combine with human error to defeat the best-laid plans of mice and men. Time served as Collins' ally in the Wilson incident. The winning number proved to be 10:30. Collins' and Gallagher's teams are gambling that 12:15 is their new lucky number.

On a typical day in Westgate Penitentiary time passes slowly, the clock ticks evenly, one day is much like another. Space is evenly divided between inside and outside space, though inside space seems finite and outside space seems infinite. But at 12:15 on the afternoon of the escape attempt, time and space rapidly converge. The sadistic Captain Munsey learns the details of the escape plan by infiltrating Collins' space through an informant. Armed guards are stationed near the outside of the tower, so the drainpipe is no longer outside space but is rejoined to the prison. The time of the escape, because it is known to Munsey, is no longer lucky for the convicts.

The barriers of time and space are rendered immaterial as the action moves at lightning speed. Gallagher begins his attack promptly at 12:15. Meanwhile, Collins and company overpower the guards in the drainpipe and head for the tower. Spencer, Lister, and Freshman are killed almost immediately and at the same time. Coy, though wounded, somehow overpowers the guards posted outside before dying himself. Soldier is killed next leaving only the wounded Collins to seize the tower and throw the lever opening the gate. Meanwhile, Munsey's machine gun is firing into the yard. Gallagher announces that the plan, so perfectly engineered, is now a "flop." Gallagher, certain that Collins has been killed and desperate to do something amidst the chaos, commandeers a truck and tries to ram the gate, even though it is still locked. Amazingly, Collins reaches the tower where he struggles against Munsey. Through superhuman effort, Collins reaches the lever, but the gate will not open. Gallagher, wounded and barely conscious behind the wheel, tries to get through but cannot. The truck is blocking the gate and the gate is blocking the truck.

The inmates of R17 were defeated by the human weakness that Collins feared but also by the cards or "fate or a jinx or whatever you want to call it." As it turned out, 12:15 proved to be most unlucky, and the perfect plan backfired perfectly. Collins and Gallagher gambled their lives on time and space and rolled snake eyes. The plan called for a perfectly timed attack using synchronized forces. Their objective was the gate, the barrier that separates inside space from outside space. The plan worked perfectly in a perverse sense. Collins' and Gallagher's attacks were perfectly synchronized. Collins reached the tower at the exact time Gallagher rammed the gate. Their escape was ultimately thwarted by the design of the barrier separating space. The gate opens into the yard toward captivity instead of out towards freedom.

Brute Force uses the penitentiary as the ultimate symbol of meaningless activity, pointless effort, doomed hope, and the torture of too much time and not enough space. The prison film is the most extreme example of the noir vision of the world. The carefully regulated structure of the penitentiary and its controlled environment would seem to undermine the sense of the randomness of existence, just as the rational ordering of society implies that life is "a clean orderly sane responsible affair." The regimentation of incarceration actually creates a different effect. The drudgery of daily activity and the pressure of prison life function to intensify the sense of the meaninglessness of existence. "Serving" time in prison is the most brutal example of slow, agonizing death. When Gallagher labels Collins' pessimistic statements "cemetery talk," Collins snaps, "We're dead ain't we? We just ain't buried." Noir protagonists are usually compulsive gamblers who would rather risk their lives in one high stakes play than die incrementally, one day at a time. The men of R17 were motivated by their desire to return to their loved ones, but they were acutely aware of the odds against a successful escape. Only minutes before the scheduled break, Dr. Walters visited the drainpipe and warned Collins that Captain Munsey knew about the time and space of the escape attempt, but Collins decided to proceed anyway. In the film's final scene, Walters tries to comprehend the seemingly irrational urge of convicts to gamble their lives against overwhelming odds.

> Why do they do it?" he asks the inmate whose wounds he is treating. "They never get away with it. Alcatraz, Atlanta, Leavenworth. It's been tried in a hundred ways from as many places. It always fails, but they keep trying. Why do they do it?

The prisoner to whom Walters poses the question, a Caribbean-American known as Calypso, has a habit of punctuating significant events with a verse of rhyming song. This time, he only shakes his head in dismay. Walters, disparagingly called a *philosopher* by one of his superiors, wants an abstract explanation, and the answer is as concrete as the walls of the penitentiary. Calypso, who experiences the ruthlessness of time and space from behind bars, explains, "Whenever you got men in prison, they're gonna want to get out."

ENDNOTES

1. Patrice allowed Helen to try on her wedding ring just before the wreck.
2. No first name is used in the film or is provided in the screenplay.
3. In *Murder, My Sweet*, Philip Marlowe, undergoing drug withdrawal, is curious about the time, only to find that his watch is missing. Never mind, he decides, "[T]hey didn't make that kind of time in watches."
4. The title of a 1948 film noir.
5. Gallagher was not interested in any escape plan until he was denied parole, which increased his time.

CHAPTER 2

THE EXISTENTIAL EPISTEMOLOGY OF NOIR

"You may *think* you know what you're dealing with."
—Noah Cross in *Chinatown*

The 1946 film noir *The Killers* begins as two tough-looking men in fedoras and tight overcoats enter opposite sides of Henry's Diner in Brentwood, New Jersey. The men order sandwiches, insult and intimidate the manager (George) and the customer (Nick), and then casually announce that they intend to shoot a man known as the Swede, living in Brentwood under the name Pete Lunn, when he enters the diner for dinner. After a while, George informs the pair that Lunn always comes to the diner before six o'clock, and since it is now after six, Lunn is not coming. The men leave, and Nick rushes to the rooming house to warn the Swede. The camera follows Nick's dark passage from the diner up to the room, where the Swede lies on his back in bed in the dark, his forearm over his face, his figure shrouded in shadows. When Nick bursts in, he and the Swede have the following exchange:

> NICK: Swede? I was over at Henry's. A couple of guys came in and tied up me and the cook, They shoved us in the kitchen. They said they were going to shoot you when you came in to supper. George thought I ought to come over and warn you.
> SWEDE: There's nothing I can do about it.
> NICK: I can tell you what they look like.
> SWEDE: I don't want to know what they're like. Thanks for coming.
> NICK: Don't you want me to go and get the police?
> SWEDE: No. That wouldn't do any good.
> NICK: Isn't there something I could do?
> SWEDE: There ain't anything to do.
> NICK: Couldn't you get out of town?
> SWEDE: No. I'm through with all that runnin' around.
> NICK: Why do they want to kill you?
> SWEDE: I did something wrong, once.

This episode involving the Swede and Nick is in many ways a definitive existential film noir scene. The Swede's reclined, solitary figure rejects offers of assistance, symbolizing the uniqueness and isolation of the individual experience. His calmly delivered response that nothing can be done, that nothing matters, demonstrates the meaninglessness of human activity in an uncaring world. The Swede's refusal to run and his remark that "I did something wrong, once," indicates the acceptance of responsibility for his acts.

The narrative structure of *The Killers* resembles that of *Citizen Kane*. The latter film, released in 1941, begins with the death of newspaper mogul Charles Foster Kane as the word "rosebud" escapes his lips as he expires. A journalist is dispatched, by a team preparing a documentary film, to discover the significance of that single word, hoping it will reveal the meaning of Kane's life. Because Kane cannot be questioned, the journalist can only interview those who knew Kane, hoping they can provide insight into the dead man's history. In *The Killers*, an insurance investigator named Riordan is similarly puzzled by the Swede's final phrase, "I did something wrong, once." The facts may explain why the Swede was killed, but Riordan is more interested to learn why the victim would passively submit to being murdered. If one is to understand a man's acts, especially those that are perplexing, one must understand the man's existence. Riordan becomes an existential detective and attempts to reweave the fabric of the Swede's life by interviewing those associated with the deceased.

Riordan has no doubt investigated many claims, but his examination of the Swede's life carries him into the noir world, which challenges notions of truth as clear, objective, and certain. Once he begins his investigation, Riordan immediately discovers the first feature of the existential epistemology of noir: the subjectivity of truth. Epistemology examines the subject's relation to the truth, and in the noir world, Riordan's ability to know the truth is dependent upon the quality of the information he receives from others. Even then, he cannot be certain about what he thinks he knows. Witness accounts are sometimes false, often narrow in perspective, and always subjective.

The Swede lived in Brentwood under an alias, so it could be that the people of Brentwood did not know the Swede at all, but only knew the identity he assumed. Nick knew the man who called himself Pete Lunn only as a coworker. George knew him only as someone who usually took his dinner at Henry's diner. Both men agree that Lunn kept to himself. Nick shares that a few days before the murder, the Swede serviced a man's car, then immediately reported feeling sick and went home, where he remained until the killers came. Nick's report cannot provide much insight into the Swede's life or explain why the Swede was murdered and refused the offer of help.

Riordan soon identifies the Swede as Ole Anderson and traces his past to Philadelphia. Riordan interviews Anderson's best friend and arresting officer, his former girlfriend, his cellmate, and a chambermaid. According to their accounts, which Riordan connects, the Swede had been a promising boxer until his right hand was permanently damaged during a fight. He soon got mixed up with certain criminals and became infatuated with a woman, Kitty Collins, who traveled in their circle. The Swede took the rap when Kitty was accused of possession of stolen property. After his release from prison, the Swede rejoined the gang and participated in a sensational robbery. The knowledge obtained from these accounts sheds no light on why the Swede was murdered or why he offered no resistance.

The information about the robbery leads Riordan to the identities of the other robbery participants, whom Riordan must interrogate to solve the riddle. Because the criminals are the only witnesses to the robbery, their testimonies are the only versions available. In separate interrogations, Blinky and DumDum, two of the thieves, report that when the crew arrived at the rendezvous after the heist, the Swede took the money at gunpoint. Riordan eventually locates "Big Jim" Colfax, the gang's former leader, now operating a construction business, and Colfax confirms Blinky's and DumDum's versions of the robbery and aftermath. This account could explain why the Swede was killed: one of the robbers found him in Brentwood and exacted revenge. But a plausible explanation is not the same as the truth. Riordan still only knows what he has been told.

Riordan accepts these accounts, but he has little choice. This version of the events is supported by the available witnesses, and therefore, it is treated as the truth. What other truth is there? If there is any such thing as the independent, objective truth, how can it be determined or obtained? This tale offered by the criminals, who may be self-serving, incriminates the Swede, and his murder is explained as street justice; he double-crossed his partners, and they killed him.

Riordan locates Kitty Collins, who admits that she and Colfax actually hoodwinked the Swede. Kitty convinced the infatuated Anderson that she would leave Colfax to be with him and also persuaded him that the gang was planning to double-cross him during the money split and that he should turn the tables. Kitty then deserted Anderson, taking the loot with her. Queenie, the chambermaid, reported that Anderson was in a rage and attempted to hurl himself through the hotel room window upon learning of Kitty's treachery. Colfax's story, combined with Kitty's and Queenie's, provides a means to understand the murder, if their versions are accepted. The other members of the gang knew Colfax and

Kitty were now married. If either of them happened upon the Swede and gave him a chance to talk, they might realize that Colfax and Kitty, not the Swede, had double-crossed them. So Colfax ordered the contract on Anderson.

However Colfax's story does not explain why the Swede offered no resistance to the killers. Riordan is left to speculate that Anderson moved to Brentwood to retreat from the world. The experience with Kitty shattered Anderson's will to live. Though he overcame the impulse to commit suicide, he was ready and willing to die and believed he deserved to die. Though he had been misled by Kitty, Anderson had betrayed the other gang members, which explains his statement, "I did something wrong, once."

The opening scene with the killers is the only portion of the story of the Swede's life that is objectively presented. The subjective stories offered by witnesses, by themselves, do not provide the entire story. Riordan *assembles the truth* from the combined statements of several observers. Are their accounts factual, complete, honest, or credible? Lubinsky and Lilly, Anderson's friends, seem sincere and genuinely sorry about what happened to Anderson. Charleston, Anderson's cellmate, is one of a few people (along with Lubinsky and Lilly) who attended Anderson's funeral. Riordan met Queenie as she returned from church carrying her Bible: Surely she would not lie. The criminals, at the time they were interrogated, had nothing to gain by lying. Whether their stories are true, half true, or mostly false, their versions of events offer a coherent narrative that provides a plausible explanation for the Swede's murder. Furthermore, in order to make sense of Anderson's passive acceptance of death, Riordan is required to selectively interpret and edit the accounts he receives and draw his own conclusion, so his subjective reading is also added to the story. At the end of the film, Riordan is confident that he has solved the mystery of the Swede. The case is officially closed, but the truth about the death and life of Ole Anderson is at least partly a subjective construction.

The presentation of truth as subjective, uncertain, elusive, and malleable is brilliantly illustrated in a scene from John Huston's film version of

The Maltese Falcon in which Brigid O'Shaunessey and Joel Cairo are getting reacquainted at Sam Spade's apartment. They have an argument that becomes violent when the buzzer sounds. Spade keeps Lt. Dundy and Sgt. Polhaus, police detectives, at the door, but when a scream is heard, they enter. When they inquire about the cut on Cairo's head, Brigid admits she struck him, but says, "I had to. I was alone in here with him. He tried to attack me. I had to keep him off. I couldn't bring myself to shoot him." Immediately Cairo jumps in. "It isn't true!" he shouts, "I came up here in good faith and then both of them attacked me. And then, when he went out to talk to you, he left her in here with a pistol and she said, as soon as you leave, they are going to kill me." When Dundy expresses his eagerness to haul them to the station, Spade cheerfully says, "Don't be in a hurry, boys. Everything can be explained." Spade tells the detectives that Brigid is "an operative in my employ," and that Cairo is an acquaintance of the deceased Thursby. According to the story Spade tells, Cairo tried to hire him to find something that Thursby possessed, but when he decided not to take the case, Cairo pulled a gun. After some discussion, he and Brigid decided to interrogate Cairo to find out how much he knew about the murders of Archer and Thursby. They may have put the questions a little roughly, Spade admits.

There are three plausible versions of the truth on the table. Brigid and Cairo were alone when Spade answered the door. Even the viewer cannot be certain about what happened, for the camera follows Spade as he greets the police detectives and remains there until they all rejoin Brigid and Cairo. Perhaps Cairo tried to attack Brigid, as she claims. Perhaps Brigid threatened to kill Cairo, as he claims. Because Spade's third version attaches Cairo to two murders, the police are confident Cairo will defend himself and tell them what *really* happened. In an effort to get at the objective truth, Dundy says, "Try telling the facts." Cairo replies, "What? Facts?" His reaction expresses that facts are not always necessary or useful for a subjective narrative.

Frustrated by the limited empirical evidence and lack of cooperation, Dundy again announces that he is taking them all downtown, and Spade tells the Lieutenant that the entire episode was a joke on the cops and then presents a fourth version of what *really* happened. "When I heard the buzzer," Spade begins, "I said to Miss O'Shaunessey and Cairo here, I said, 'They're getting to be a nuisance. When you hear them going, one of you scream and then we'll see how far we can string them before they tumble.'" Dundy asks about the cut on Cairo's head. "Maybe he cut himself shaving," Spade answers. "No," Cairo offers, "when we pretended to be struggling for the gun, I fell over the carpet. I fell."

Brigid watched with amused admiration as Spade improvised his explanation. Cairo sat dumbfounded until he realized Spade's story would probably free them from a trip to the police station. "Aw, horsefeathers," was Polhaus' skeptical reaction. Nevertheless, the story is as plausible as it is absurd. The hard fact is that Dundy and Polhaus were not present during the incident, so their knowledge of the truth is limited to the information provided by the eyewitnesses. Spade's final version, agreed to by all members who were present, for it keeps them out of trouble, fulfills his promise that "everything can be explained." If Dundy takes them downtown and the trio adheres to the tale, the police have no means to contradict their version of the truth. Ultimately, the truth becomes that which they are forced to accept. There is no available truth independent of the testimony of the participants. Spade states the matter directly in Hammett's novel, as he tells the cops he does not care whether they believe his story or not. "The point is that that's our story and we'll stick to it," he says, "The newspapers will print it whether they believe it or not, and it'll be just as funny one way as the other, or more so. What are you going to do about it? It's no crime to kid a copper, is it? You haven't got anything on anybody here. Everything we told you was part of the joke. What are you going to do about it?" (Hammett, *Maltese Falcon* 458)

Spade, the experienced existentialist detective, is fully aware that the seeker of knowledge is dependent upon the subjective version of the storyteller. Towards the end of the film, Spade asks Gutman for a summary of events pertaining to two deaths so that he (Spade) can "be sure the parts that don't fit can be covered up," and the story is coherent, whether or not objectively accurate, when reported to the police.

Sam Spade appears in every scene of *The Maltese Falcon*,[1] and the narrative unfolds through his perspective. The viewer experiences the mystery with Spade, learns what Spade learns through Spade's sources of information, and experiences Spade's difficulties. Spade's knowledge of the falcon, the valuable statuette at the center of the story, is limited to the information he receives from Caspar Gutman, who assures Spade that if Brigid and Cairo do not know what the falcon is, then "I'm the only one in the whole wide, sweet world who does." If Gutman is the only person who knows, or if the others concede that they do not know, then there is no version of the truth except his. As Gutman relates his tale of the falcon, he tells Spade, "These are facts, historical facts; not schoolbook history, not Mr. Well's history, but history nevertheless." The statement implies that Gutman's version, which may be a subjective *his*tory, is as legitimate as the recorded history on the subject. When they turn to the estimated value of the falcon, Gutman says, "Well, sir, if I told you half, you'd call me a liar." Gutman is presented as a learned man, a credible source, and the viewer has no reason to doubt the accuracy of his account, which may or may not be true. Spade replies that he would not call Gutman a liar, even if he thought so. There is no basis for Spade to challenge Gutman's assessment, for only Gutman can establish the truth.

The viewer's ability to appreciate the subjective nature of knowledge was enhanced in two noir films that employed a subjective camera and limited the viewer's visual field to the perspective of the protagonist. Advertisements for *The Lady in the Lake* (1947) invited the audience to experience the investigation and solve the crime along with Private Detective Philip Marlowe. The subjective camera was put to better use in a better film noir, *Dark Passage* (1947). The technique was applied to overcome the difficulty involved with the protagonist's plastic surgery. Instead of hiring another actor to play escaped convict Vincent Parry for the first part of the film, the studio operated the subjective camera to hide Humphrey Bogart's image until Parry received his new face through plastic surgery.

Dark Passage opens with a view of San Quentin Penitentiary and the surrounding area. We next see an outbound prison truck transporting barrels, with a pair of hands over the edge of a barrel. The barrel is rocked off the truck and the camera's perspective is relocated to its inside. As the barrel rolls downhill, our (and Parry's) perspective is reoriented and disoriented. Suddenly, our view of the world and knowledge of the world is restricted to what is available to Parry. The scene is no longer panoramic and omniscient, but limited and constricted. The atmosphere is tense because of Parry's dangerous escape attempt, but the anxiety is heightened because the subjective camera controls the range of perception and knowledge. The opening shot gives comfort that the whole world, or at least the world around San Quentin, is available to our faculties. By reducing the visual field to the inside of the barrel, we are made aware of how insufficient and inadequate our knowledge can be. We may reason that the world we knew only a moment ago remains as it was, but Parry's desperate condition forces us to realize how little we can declare with certainty about that world.

When the French philosopher Rene Descartes decided to determine what he could know with certainty, he retired to the privacy of his chamber, donned his dressing gown, and implemented his radical doubt methodology. In the opening chapter of *Meditations on First Philosophy*, he explains that all his knowledge was to be doubted because it had come from the senses, which are deceptive. The objects of the world are also to be doubted because knowledge of them is obtained through the deceptive senses. Descartes looks at his own hand and questions whether he is actually looking at his hand. Perhaps he is being deceived by an evil demon. Perhaps it is all a dream. Before long, Descartes doubts his very existence. There is, however, one thing Descartes can know with certainty: the thoughts he is experiencing. Even if the demon is confusing his thoughts, Descartes is still having thoughts. At the very least, he is a thinking thing. Eventually, Descartes confirms his existence through his own mental conceptions, through the clear and distinct impressions of his mind. In order to discover what he can know with certainty, Descartes determines that he must withdraw from lived experience in the world, which is the realm of deception and falsehood.

Descartes' process of radical doubt strikes the noir existential epistemologist as artificial. If Descartes' radical doubt is genuine, no complicated methodology is needed. There is a quick and easy way for
Descartes to test the validity of his existence: He can put a gun to his
head and slowly squeeze the trigger. At that point, the existential epistemologist is confident that Descartes' faith in his existence and the reality
of the gun will be restored. The extreme situations presented in hard-
boiled fiction and film noir illustrate that knowledge and action are connected and have existential consequences. Eccentric claims about doubt
and certainty are likely to be modified when life and death immediately
hang in the balance. In *Dark Passage*, Vincent Parry hears the prison
siren, which means his escape has been discovered. He calculates that
he has approximately fifteen minutes before the authorities catch and
inspect the prison truck and retrace their steps in an organized search
of the area. Parry does not have a theoretical problem, but a concrete
one. Parry must act quickly, but if he proceeds beyond the bounds of his
knowledge, he risks his freedom and perhaps his life. Soon Parry says,
"I've got to start taking chances," indicating that he must proceed. He
would like to be certain considering the stakes, but given his existential condition, he cannot be more confident about his knowledge of the
world beyond his limited scope.

Descartes and his rationalist comrades seek knowledge of "a clean
orderly sane responsible" sort. They conclude that knowledge cannot be
generated by the physical world, which is unstable, irrational, and contingent. They escape, one might say, into the "clean orderly sane responsible" realm of the mind. Descartes' successful operation confirms the
viability of human reason as the means to knowledge, validates scientific inquiry, and affirms the world and human life as the products of a
perfect God. The existential epistemologist of noir accepts Descartes'
premise that the physical world is a problematic source of knowledge,
especially if one seeks knowledge that is transcendent, objective, and
certain. But noir existentialism reaches a different, unsettling conclusion: There is no escape to any other world, including the world of the
mind. Noir lends a pessimistic twist to the notion of the subjectivity of

truth in films like *Dark Passage* because the protagonist's subjectivity is a source of anxiety. Vincent Parry's subjective experience does not provide the abstract certainty and security of the mind. Parry must view the world from the perspective of a fugitive, and that world threatens him at every turn. He cannot know whether freedom or capture lies over the next hill or around the next corner. Each person he sees and those who see him must be judged a potential threat.

Existential epistemology neither seeks nor finds comforting solutions to the problems of knowledge in the concrete world. It resists the urge to explain existence, which is too unstable, nonrational, and contingent to be captured in the mind's conceptual constructions, but instead tries to describe it.[2] The existentialist detective does not develop a theory or concept of crime but investigates a specific crime involving specific individuals and circumstances. If he is to get to the bottom of things, the detective must go where the clues lead; he must accurately record and evaluate the concrete data. In this sense, existential epistemology is radically empirical.

Dashiell Hammett's novel *The Glass Key* (1935) follows Ned Beaumont's[3] investigation into the murder of Taylor Henry, which he undertakes to clear his friend who is suspected of the crime. The book opens with the following description of a dice game. "Green dice rolled across the green table, struck the rim together, and bounced back. One stopped short holding six white spots in two equal rows uppermost. The other tumbled out to the center of the table and came to rest with a single spot on top" (Hammett, *Glass Key* 591). Hammett's *The Maltese Falcon* contains a passage that traces the activity of discharged cigarette particles. "Ragged grey flakes of cigarette-ash dotted the yellow top of the desk and the green blotter and the papers that were there. A buff-curtained window, eight or ten inches open let in from the court a current of air faintly scented with ammonia. The ashes on the desk twitched and crawled on the current" (Hammett, *Maltese Falcon* 392). These passages offer clean and crisp descriptions of the movements of inanimate objects. The accounts are detailed yet economical. The radical empiricism of noir provides similar presentations of events involving human beings.

The following excerpt from Hammett's *Red Harvest* describes the Continental Op, a private detective, as he awakens from the first good night's sleep he has had in days.

> I opened my eyes in the dull light of morning sun filtered through drawn blinds. I was lying face down on the dining room floor, my head resting on my left forearm. My right arm was stretched straight out. My right hand held the round blue and white handle of Dinah Brand's ice pick. The pick's six-inch needle-sharp blade was buried in Dinah Brand's left breast. (Hammett, *Red Harvest* 142–143).

This description is remarkable for its neutral presentation of a woman's corpse. There is no abrupt transition from the report of the morning sun to the dead body because, to the neutral eye, there is no difference. The chapter title, "The Seventeenth Murder," coolly announces that killing is routine, and the incident is described with the humdrum attitude of a man accustomed to violent death.

These matter-of-fact statements of events, whether they involve rolling dice or scattering ashes or a corpse, are characteristic of noir's hard-boiled sensibility and its radically empirical approach to knowledge. The accounts are those of a neutral reporter, and seem "hard-boiled" because they are devoid of sentimental language. There is no omniscient observer to explain the *why* of matters, only the *what* is offered. The narration, whether first person or third person, does not operate from a privileged position, and claims to knowledge are limited to that which is observable from the distance the narration must maintain as an uninvited guest. The narrator has no more access to the inner workings of human beings and their affairs than of inanimate objects. For all it knows, the movements of human beings and inanimate objects are indistinguishable.

The private detective is an essential figure in any discussion of noir epistemology because he is a professional investigator. He is an expert in acquiring knowledge, and he is ultimately investigating people. The inability to know what lies beneath the surface is an impediment to the noir detective's attempt to solve the case. The deception and falsehood of the noir world take the form of the characters he encounters. The noir detective's neutral observations and deadpan reportage reflects his awareness of the existential limitations of knowledge, but the noir detective regards himself as *a most wised-up guy* and prides himself on his ability to not only see, but see through, the deception and falsehood of the inhabitants of his world.

The conflict involved in the detective's need to evaluate others and the empirical limits he accepts are played out in Sam Spade's relationship with Brigid O'Shaunessey in *The Maltese Falcon*. Brigid, using the name Wonderly, hired Spade and Archer to locate her missing sister, who she claimed was keeping company with a man named Floyd Thursby. Brigid agreed to meet Thursby that evening to enable Archer to follow them to the sister. Now that Thursby and Archer are dead, Brigid admits to Spade that the story she told the detectives was false. She tells Spade that she desperately needs his help but must withhold information about herself and her affairs. Brigid begs Spade to trust her, and in order to proceed with confidence, Spade must determine whether she is now telling the truth. Spade's task is overwhelmingly difficult if he bases his judgment on empirical knowledge.

In the following extended passage from Hammett's novel, Brigid delivers an entreaty that illustrates Spade's dilemma:

> I've been bad—worse than you could know—but I'm not all bad. Look at me, Mr. Spade. You know I'm not all bad, don't you? You can see that, can't you? Then can't you trust me just a little? Oh, I'm so alone and afraid, and I've got nobody to help me if you won't help me. I know I've no right to ask you to trust me if I won't trust you. I do trust you, but I can't tell you. I can't tell you now. Later I will, when I can. I'm afraid, Mr. Spade. I'm afraid of trusting you. I don't mean that. I do trust you, but— I trusted Floyd and—I've nobody else, Mr. Spade. You can help me. You've said you can help me. If I hadn't believed you could save me I would have run away today instead of sending for you. If I thought anybody else could save me would I be down on my knees like this? (*Maltese Falcon* 418–419)

Brigid says "*Look* at me." and "You *know* I'm not all bad, don't you?" and "You can *see* that, can't you?" (my italics) as though her words and actions during this meeting provide empirical evidence of her sincerity and the truth of her statements.

The narrative reports no thoughts from Spade about Brigid's earnestness. In empirical fashion, we learn his attitudes from his words. After hearing her speech, Spade remarks, "You won't need much of anybody's help. You're good. You're very good. It's chiefly in your eyes, I think, and that throb you get into your voice when you say things like 'Be generous, Mr. Spade.'" Brigid replies that "the lie was in the way I said it, and not at all in what I said." Brigid's words imply that if Spades suspends whatever bias he may have due to her previous lie, and neutrally evaluates her based on the current empirical evidence, he should be able to *see* and *know* that she is not all bad. "Look at me," she seems to say, "and tell me whether you can honestly say I'm all bad." In other words, appearances are accurate measures of truth. On the other hand, by admitting that the "lie" was in the way she delivered her speech, not in its content, Brigid implies that appearances are deceiving.

Brigid acknowledges that Spade's suspicion and frustration are justified because she is concealing information about her affairs. Her claim that Spade should be able to know and see the truth is based on her efforts not to conceal but to reveal her fears. Brigid may not be speaking the whole truth, but the language of her body cannot lie, can it? Indeed the narrative reports Brigid as nervous and fidgety. She blushes, cries, and even drops to her knees as she pleads for Spade's help. Spade asks several questions, hoping to learn enough to allow him to proceed with confidence and receives limited and unsatisfactory answers. He finally says, "This is hopeless," and "I can't do anything for you. I don't know what you want done. I don't even know if you know what you want." Brigid answers, "You've been patient. You've tried to help me. It is hopeless, and useless, I suppose," and in conclusion, "I thank you for what you have done. I—I'll have to take my chances" (Hammett, *Maltese Falcon* 422). Is Brigid genuinely resigned to Spade quitting the case, or is she being manipulative, playing the role of the damsel in distress?

The empirical messages are conflicting, and even Spade seems uncertain about how to interpret Brigid's actions. Should he trust his senses or bring intuitive impressions and attitudes to bear? He can decide that she is being manipulative, but what would be the basis for that judgment? Would Spade be interpreting her behavior using his experience and biases about clients? The empirical data provide information but cannot tell him how to interpret that data. The exchanges between Spade and Brigid illustrate the limitations of the radical empiricist approach to knowledge. Yes, Brigid seems nervous. Is she agitated because she is a victim too frightened to reveal what she knows, or is she worried because the truth would incriminate her? It is not enough to know the facts, whatever those might be; Spade must ascertain the meaning of the facts, and radical empiricism will not provide that meaning.

Realizing that the empirical data are not sufficient, Spade becomes direct and asks, "You aren't exactly the sort of person you pretend to be, are you?" Spade reminds Brigid that her admission that she has been bad, "worse than you could know," contains the exact words and tone that she offered at their last meeting. "It's a speech you've practiced," Spade tells her. Brigid acknowledges her duplicity but remarks that her behavior is "a pose I've grown into, so you won't expect me to drop it entirely, will you?" (Hammett, *Maltese Falcon* 436–437). Brigid's apparent candor further complicates Spade's ability to know. Her admission that she will sometimes lie does not facilitate understanding but further obscures Spade's ability to interpret the meaning of her words.

Later in the story, in the comfort of Spade's apartment, he attempts to extract information from Brigid about the falcon. Brigid tells a tale about her partnership with Floyd Thursby and Joel Cairo and relates how she and Cairo acquired the falcon and were double-crossed by Thursby. When she finishes, Spade asks, "Was there any truth in that yarn?" Brigid replies, "Some. Not—not very much." Spade can only ask because there was no way for him to really know. Brigid then lays back and says, "Oh, I'm so tired of it all, of myself, of lying and thinking up lies, and of not knowing what is a lie and what is the truth. I wish I..." (Hammett, *Maltese Falcon* 467). The narrative provides the following report of their physical activity: "She put her hands up to Spade's cheeks, put her open mouth hard against his mouth, her body flat against his body," and "Spade's arms went around her, holding her to him, muscles bulging his blue sleeves, a hand cradling her head, its fingers half lost among red hair, a hand moving groping fingers over her slim back" (Hammett, *Maltese Falcon* 467).

Again, Spade has the same dilemma. Was Brigid sincere about her desire to find someone to trust, someone with whom she could relax and unburden herself? Is she really in danger? Is her admission another tactic to enlist Spade's trust? Is her sexual desire for Spade genuine or simply a technique for maintaining his aid? How are her actions to be interpreted if the empirical evidence is regarded neutrally? Are there certain actions that objectively demonstrate sincerity? Knowledge is often the basis for decision-making but is frequently also used to remove the burden and responsibility of decision-making. Knowledge provides information but cannot make the decision. Knowing more, if he indeed knows more, does not solve Spade's difficulties.

By the end of the story, Spade has still not deciphered Brigid. She confesses under duress that she killed Miles Archer but pleads with Spade not to "send her over" because they love each other. Does she love him? Brigid admits that she has not "played square" with Spade for "half an hour at a stretch," yet she tells him that, "You're lying if you say you don't know down in your heart that, in spite of anything I've done, that I love you" (Hammett, *Maltese Falcon* 580). Brigid's statement asserts that her words and deeds are not indicative of her true feelings, which means the empirical evidence is not to be trusted. Just as the Swede's life was greater than the sum of the accumulated subjective stories, she wants Spade to believe that her feelings are greater than the expressions offered by the data. Brigid may be correct, but what other evidence is there? Spade confesses that he does not know and does not have the means to determine whether Brigid loves him or whether he loves her.

The limitations of radical empiricism instruct us that we cannot know others, not really. People are too complex (and deceitful) to be interpreted solely from empirical data, but the existential epistemologist recognizes the legitimacy of empirical boundaries. To do otherwise is to claim access to other persons that we do not have. Spade can use other means to determine whether Brigid loves him, but he must concede that these means will not provide the certainty that rationalists demand. As a principled existential detective, Spade acknowledges that he does not know, even though an assertion of knowledge would make his decision easier. If Brigid is telling the truth about her love for Spade, even as she admits she has not "played square" with him, it is fair to conclude that her behavior is inconsistent with the feelings she expresses. Through the faithful practice of empiricism, the noir existential detective encounters the third barrier to investigation in the noir world, which is the inability to fully comprehend and explain human behavior.

Conventional police investigations begin with the presumption of human rationality. In the neo-noir *The Usual Suspects* (1995), Verbal Kint shares police philosophy. "To a cop," he says to Special Agent Kujan, "the explanation is never that complicated. It's always simple. There's no mystery to the street, no arch criminal behind it all. If you've got a dead body and you think his brother did it, you're going to find out you're right." Kujan tells Kint, "First day on the job, you know what I learned? How to spot a murderer. Let's say you arrest three guys for the same killing. You put them in jail overnight. The next morning, whoever's sleeping is your man. You see, if you're guilty, you know you're caught, you get some rest; you let your guard down." According to Kint, Kujan, and police philosophy, human beings are always rational creatures whose motives and actions are not complicated but are simple and transparent.

In the noir, world human beings are highly complex and largely opaque to others. In *The Maltese Falcon*, Sam Spade could not be certain whether Brigid loves him. In *Criss Cross*, Steve Thompson participates in an armored car robbery to acquire money to run away with his avaricious ex-wife, Anna, now married to gangster Slim Dundee. After the robbery, Anna (who has the money) waits at the cottage as the couple planned, but when the injured Thompson arrives late, he finds Anna annoyed that he got there before she could get away. Anna had pursued Thompson and married Dundee only after Lt. Ramirez, at the behest of Thompson's mother, warned her to stay away. In both cases, and several more that could be cited, the protagonists cannot read these women who, based on the empirical data, seem greedy and corrupt, but also appear sincere about their love.

Sam Spade conceded his inability to accurately read Brigid O'Shaunessey, but his immediate acceptance of the obstacles to investigation posed by the opaqueness of others is unusual among noir protagonists. Spade declined to make a judgment that required more knowledge than he had. He does not leap to conclusions and therefore does not reach false conclusions. Spade could not know whether Gutman was honest in his account of the falcon, so he did not challenge it. He did not, and could not, know whether Brigid loved him; therefore, he did not factor that issue into his decision. Spade learned that Brigid had, in fact, killed Miles Archer, so when the police arrived, he unceremoniously handed her over. More often, the noir private detective must learn the hard way that he does not and cannot know what others are thinking and feeling, whether they are honest or dishonest, virtuous or corrupt. When the noir detective makes such judgments he is almost always wrong, and he and his clients suffer the consequences.

In *Chinatown* (1974), private detective J. J. ("call me Jake") Gittes is unable to penetrate the exteriors of those he encounters, though he believes he knows them. Gittes fails in each case because he does not respect the boundaries of empiricism that Spade recognizes and instead substitutes his biases for neutral, accurate reporting. Gittes specializes in what he refers to as "matrimonial work," or infidelity cases, and he is confident that his experience in such matters gives him special insight into human nature. Furthermore, Gittes is generally cynical about people and their affairs (pun intended), and when in doubt, he applies his attitude that people are always motivated by selfish interests. In *The Maltese Falcon*, Spade was hindered by the masks others wore that he had no means to penetrate. *Chinatown* effectively illustrates that the opaqueness of human beings can be enhanced by the investigator's projection onto others. Gittes cannot accurately read those involved in the case, if that were even possible, because their exteriors are imposed by his internally generated characterizations.

Gittes' inability to see the person presented to him is observed in the film's second scene, when a client introduces herself as Evelyn Mulwray. She wants Gittes to investigate her suspicion that her husband, Hollis Mulwray, is having an affair. Mulwray is chief engineer of the city's Department of Water and Power. Unfortunately, the woman requesting services is not actually Evelyn Mulwray, but an impostor. Ida Sessions, a self-described "working girl" hired to impersonate Evelyn Mulwray, is dressed in the type of outfit a rich woman might wear: tailored black suit, pillbox hat with veil, pearl necklace, black gloves, and diamond bracelet. She uses a cigarette holder, affects an air, tells Gittes that money is no object, and the effect is complete. Ida Sessions does not look at all like Evelyn Mulwray, but she fits the image Gittes has formed of the rich wife seeking his services. In a sense, it does not matter whether she is Evelyn Mulwray; her specific identity is unimportant. She appears as a rich woman with a philandering husband and money to spend, and Gittes treats her accordingly. Later in the film, Ida Sessions phones and identifies herself honestly, and Gittes mocks her for the benefit of his associates. Unable to see her, Gittes does not mistake her for a rich client and does not project that identity onto her.

Gittes also fails to see beyond the image he creates of Hollis Mulwray. Gittes spends the first day of the investigation following Mulwray to a city council meeting, the L. A. River Bed, and then to Point Fermin Park. Duffy, Gittes' associate, phones to say he has located Mulwray with his mistress at Echo Park. Gittes photographs Mulwray and the young lady at a secluded hotel, and the next day, the pictures appear in the newspaper under the sensational headline: Department of Water and Power Blows Fuse Over Chief's Use of Funds for El Macanda Love Nest. The real Evelyn Mulwray appears at Gittes' office with her attorney, and Gittes realizes he has been duped. Nevertheless, Gittes is still certain that Mulwray is a cheating spouse and is determined to confirm his judgment. He speaks with Mulwray's deputy, Russell Yelburton, who tells Gittes, "You work with a man a certain length of time, you come to know him, his habits, his values, and so forth. Well, either he's the kind who chases after women or he isn't." "He never even kids about it," Yelburton adds. "Maybe he takes it very seriously," Gittes leers.

Gittes is completely mistaken about Hollis Mulwray, but he is at this stage certain about his assessment. Even though he spent an entire day following Mulwray and saw no romantic or sexual activity, and even though Mulwray's closest professional associate discounts the charge, Gittes remains certain about his knowledge because he has projected the cheating husband image onto Mulwray. His evidence of infidelity consists of two sets of photographs, those he took at the hotel and those he and Duffy took at Echo Park. The empirical data, neutrally examined, merely show Mulwray and Kathryn together on two occasions. The cheating husband is applied by Gittes, whose prejudice against Mulwray supplies the adultery through his subjective interpretation of the evidence.

Gittes is also completely wrong in his reading of Mulwray's alleged girlfriend, whom he describes to Evelyn Mulwray as "pretty, in a cheap sort of way, of course." Gittes has mostly observed the "girlfriend" through a telephoto lens, but he is certain about her character. The young lady in question is not Mulwray's girlfriend at all but is the innocent product of an incestuous affair between Evelyn Mulwray and her father, Noah Cross. Katherine, the young girl, is approximately fifteen years old and Hollis Mulwray was meeting her secretly to shield her identity and location. During the rowboat scenes at Echo Park and at the El Macando Arms hotel, Katherine is dressed and groomed like a delicate young miss. When Gittes photographs her at the hotel, she is merely showing off her pretty new dress, perfectly appropriate for a girl her age. The picture of her modeling the dress appears in the paper under a scandalous headline. Despite Katherine's innocence, Gittes is unable to see her real self under the mask of the cheap mistress he has applied to her.

Gittes is most unable to effectively see Evelyn Mulwray. Throughout much of the film, Evelyn Mulwray remains for Gittes the character Ida Sessions impersonated. Even after it is revealed that the woman was an impostor and Evelyn Mulwray never actually hired Gittes to spy on her husband, Gittes continues to treat Evelyn Mulwray as a woman angered by her husband's infidelity. When Mulwray is found murdered, Gittes suspects Evelyn Mulwray because her husband's alleged affair gives her a motive. Even after she hires Gittes to investigate her husband's death, he remains suspicious because he cannot shake his perception of her. During a single afternoon and evening, Evelyn Mulwray assists Gittes' charade at the Mar Vista Inn and Rest Home, helps him escape a pair of thugs, treats his wounded nose, and they make love. Nevertheless, when Evelyn receives a call and tells Gittes she has to leave and asks him to wait and trust her, he follows her to where she is concealing Katherine. Because they have been intimate, Gittes is willing to be more charitable in his assessment of Evelyn, but his analysis of the crime still bears his conviction that she killed her husband and is holding his mistress hostage. Gittes tells her, "I'll make it easy. You were jealous, you fought, he fell, hit his head. It was an accident, but his girl is a witness. You've had to pay her off. You don't have the stomach to harm her, but you've got the money to shut her up."

Evelyn Mulwray is indeed nervous and agitated during their meetings, which fuels Gittes' suspicions, but her anxiety has nothing to do with her marital relations. She is desperately trying to protect Katherine from the clutches of Noah Cross, who is using his powerful connections to search for the girl. Evelyn was fifteen when she had sexual relations with her father, and Katherine appears to be approximately that age. Evelyn Mulwray is actually the only major character in the film operating from selfless motives, but Gittes is unable to consider any other explanation for her behavior because he clings to his original characterization of her.

Gittes is unable to correctly read the face of Noah Cross. When they first meet and Cross asks "What exactly do you know about me, Mr. Gittes?" Gittes answers, "Mainly that you're rich and too respectable to want your name in the papers." Cross grins, "Of course I'm respectable. I'm old. Politicians, ugly buildings and whores all get respectable if they last long enough." Actually, Gittes knows next to nothing about Cross. If he did, he would know that Cross is anything but respectable. Gittes does not know that Cross is guilty of the statutory rape of Evelyn.

He does not know that Cross is currently searching for Katherine and that he hired Ida Sessions hoping that Gittes' investigation would lead him to the girl. He does not know that Cross murdered Hollis Mulwray. Gittes does not even know that Cross is Evelyn's father until she admits it. Cross accurately tells Gittes, "You may *think* you know what you're dealing with, but, believe me, you don't." Gittes does not suspect Cross because he has projected the identity of the harmless old man onto Cross.

Cross tells Gittes, "[M]ost people never have to face the fact that at the right place and right time, they're capable of anything." If Cross is correct, others must remain opaque because their virtually unlimited possibilities make it almost impossible for us to read them or know them. The labels we apply can never truly be accurate, except perhaps temporarily, and are generally misleading. A person who has always been easygoing and gentle could suddenly become temperamental and violent. Sam Spade's understanding of Cross' lesson enabled him to solve Miles Archer's murder in *The Maltese Falcon*. The forensic evidence indicated that Archer's killer stood close to him, and Archer's gun was in his holster, and his overcoat was buttoned. In order to suspect Brigid, Spade must realize that she is capable of hiring a detective in the afternoon, leading him down a dark alley that night, standing close as though to kiss him, then firing a shot into his heart. Unless Spade is willing to believe Brigid capable of such actions, he does not suspect her. Spade's ability to suspend judgment and consider all possibilities has personal costs, but he correctly solves the case of his partner's murder.

The images Gittes projects onto Evelyn Mulwray and Noah Cross achieve permanence, and his actions have dire consequences for Katherine and fatal consequences for Evelyn. Gittes cannot resist confronting Cross about what he knows, and he again underestimates the *old* man. Cross and his henchman force Gittes to take them to where the women are hiding in Chinatown. Gittes hurriedly tries to explain to the police that Cross is "the bird you're after," but the image of the respectable patriarch is now fixed. The police also believe, thanks to Gittes, that Evelyn killed her husband and is holding his mistress hostage. She is considered a fugitive and is shot trying to escape. As the police stand by, Cross pulls the terrified Katherine away from her dead mother and introduces himself as her "grandfather." Gittes' misjudgment illustrates the deceptiveness of confident claims to know. The subject brings his own prejudices, or theory of the case, to the evidence. The objects of knowledge are also problematic, for they are not what they seem to be, and are sometimes deliberately misleading. Under these conditions, the protagonist who claims to know only deceives himself and endangers others.

Gittes is affected by the tragic outcome in *Chinatown* because he eventually comes to care about the human lives entangled in the case. The existential noir detective is not involved in the pursuit of knowledge *for the sake of knowledge*. Knowledge has no sake: Human beings have values and purposes. The detective has reasons for wanting to know, and the quest has personal significance. In *The Killers*, Riordan feels compelled to discover and understand the Swede's passive acceptance of death even though the insurance claim is not at stake. Gittes is determined to investigate the Mulwray infidelity case even after Evelyn agrees to drop the lawsuit because "I'm not the one who's supposed to be caught with his pants down," he explains. Evelyn is moved to ask Gittes, "Is this a business or an obsession with you?" That is not to say that the detective does not take many unimportant cases out of the necessity to earn a living. In such instances, he plods along, gathering evidence until the client's issues are resolved. Hard-boiled fiction and film noir do not present these standard cases, though they are obviously part of the detective's history. The stories shared with readers and viewers are those with special impact or meaning to the detective.

Lost amidst the competition for the Maltese falcon is the investigation into the murder of Sam Spade's partner, Miles Archer. Throughout most of the story, Spade's words and actions do not indicate that he has much interest in solving his partner's murder. In Huston's film, Spade only briefly visits the scene of the crime. Police Sergeant Polhaus says, "It's tough him getting it like that. Miles had his faults, but I guess he must have had some good points too." Spade's only response is to mutter, "I guess so." Spade instructs his secretary, Effie, to break the bad news to Archer's wife, Iva. Effie reports that Iva had just returned home and had mussed her apartment to make it appear she had been home all night, and Spade tells her, "You're a detective, darling, but she didn't kill him." The matter is dropped, and Spade concludes their conversation telling Effie to have Archer's desk moved out of the office and his name removed from the doors and windows. When Brigid expresses grief over Archer's murder, Spade tells her "Stop it. He knew what he was doing. Those are the chances we take." Brigid asks whether Archer was married and Spade says, "Yeah, with ten thousand insurance, no children, and a wife that didn't like him," then adds, "Anyway, there's no time for worrying about that now." Archer's murder is discussed only once more before the end of the film, when the police learn about Spade's affair with Iva and visit the detective's apartment to ask about it. The line of inquiry is interrupted when Cairo's scream is heard and the police are led through the farce described earlier.

It would seem that solving Archer's murder has little meaning for Spade, but his showdown with Brigid, which occurs after matters concerning the falcon are settled, proves otherwise. Spade has discovered that Brigid is Archer's murderer, and it is possible he has known since early in the case. When he confronts her with his evidence of her guilt, Brigid's only defense is that Spade ought to spare her. "Surely Mr. Archer wasn't as much to you as...," she sobs. Brigid does not realize that Archer's significance is not individual, but symbolic, and Spade's need to resolve his partner's murder goes to the very heart of what it means to be a detective, and being a detective is at the center of Spade's personal sense of identity.

Spade begins his lengthy explanation to Brigid, telling her, "This won't do any good, but I'll try it once and then give it up," indicating that his reasons are individual and personal, and perhaps inexplicable. Spade and Archer were partners, and "when a man's partner is killed you're supposed to do something. It doesn't make any difference what you thought of him, he was your partner and you're supposed to do something," he informs her. "When one of your organization gets killed," Spade continues, "It's bad business to let the killer get away with it, bad all around, bad for every detective everywhere." In other words, a detective is more than a person with a license to investigate. A private detective is a member of an organization of men who have chosen their profession and are committed to its responsibilities. The private detective's life contains no family, lasting affairs with women, or noteworthy friendships. He must usually scrape for work, and his economic status is modest. His relations with the official agents of law enforcement are often antagonistic. The detective's clients are frequently untrustworthy and the information he is given can be incomplete, inaccurate, or deliberately misleading. He may be required to risk limb and life for the meager pay he receives. But the life of the private detective contains one characteristic that makes his sacrifice and suffering acceptable: autonomy. If killers of detectives are allowed to get away with it, soon there would be no detectives, and one of the few professions that provide autonomous employment to working-class men would be eliminated.

Hard-boiled fiction and film noir present cases that have special meaning for the investigators, but these cases invariably end in failure, which contributes to their sense of frustration, impotence, and pessimism. Knowledge, long considered the foundation of truth and wisdom for many philosophers, provides information but cannot live up to its promise to answer all questions and solve all problems. In *The Maltese Falcon*, Spade ultimately acquires the falcon, but the statuette is a fake, symbolizing the futility of the activity. Spade uncovers the murderer of his partner, but that discovery requires that he choose between the woman he may love and his responsibilities as a professional. Though the choice is clear for Spade, the consequences are nevertheless painful, and he admits he will have "some rotten nights" after turning Brigid over to the police. Furthermore, Spade is forced to admit to himself that he may love a woman capable of lying and cheating and killing in cold blood. Hammett's novel ends as Iva Archer, the mistress Spade now wishes he had "never laid eyes on,"[4] waits in his outer office. In addition to everything else that has gone wrong, Spade is still not rid of her. The knowledge Spade acquires in the case confirms his cynical attitude that people are corrupt, and human activity is ultimately meaningless.

There are two narratives presented in *The Killers*: the Swede's and Riordan's. The Swede's narrative ends with his death: Riordan's narrative pertains to his investigation of the insurance case. Riordan learns about the Prentiss Hat Company robbery in which $254,912.00 was stolen and never recovered. Atlantic Casualty insured Prentiss, and Riordan is excited by the opportunity to recover the money. The case becomes so important to Riordan that he threatens to quit whenever his boss, Kenyon, tries to pull him off the case. When Riordan solves the mystery and locates the money, Kenyon is not impressed and deems Riordan's investigation a waste of time and effort. "You know the insurance business," Kenyon begins, "The losses in any one year determine the premium to be paid the following. Owing to your splendid efforts, the basic rate of the Atlantic Casualty Company as of 1947 will probably drop one-tenth of a cent." Kenyon offers Riordan a reward commensurate with his achievement: Riordan can take the weekend off.

In *Dark Passage*, Vincent Parry's need to know has special meaning because he hopes to identify his wife's murderer, prove his innocence, and free himself. Along the way, Parry's best friend, George Felsinger, with whom Parry intended to stay while recovering from plastic surgery, is murdered. Parry accidentally kills Baker, a man who recognizes him and attempts blackmail. Parry eventually discovers that Madge Rapf, former lover and antagonist, is his wife's murderer. When he confronts her, Madge plunges out of the window to her death, killing Parry's evidence. *Dark Passage* ends as Parry, now living in Peru, is reunited with Irene Jansen, who enters the nightclub as the band plays their favorite song. Irene aided Parry's escape, provided shelter and support, and the couple fell in love. But this romantic and happy ending is severely undermined by the circumstances. Parry's surgical makeover does not alter the fact that he remains a fugitive who cannot return to his native country. Felsinger, Baker, and Madge are dead, and the police probably believe Parry is the murderer. Parry's purposeful investigation and search for knowledge did not solve his troubles but stripped away his identity and permanently destroyed his freedom.

In *Chinatown*, Gittes is haunted by an episode from his past in which he tried to help a woman, but his efforts only ensured that she was hurt. Once Gittes finally realizes that Evelyn is not the perpetrator, but a victim, the case that he accepted simply for money and publicity takes on personal significance. Gittes' discovery of the truth does not enable him to help the women, and his actions actually accelerate their ruin. Gittes is eager to confront Cross, to tell him what he knows, but Gittes' knowledge works against him when he is forced to reveal the women's whereabouts. He cannot convince the police, who refuse to listen because they believe that he is aiding a murder suspect. Evelyn is shot by Detective Loach, and the shocked Gittes is led away by his partners as another woman he tried to help is instead harmed.

The experience of hard-boiled fiction and film noir protagonists undermines the notion of knowledge as objective and certain and the source of power and meaning. The noir detective experiences the limitations of subjectivity and empiricism and is frustrated by his inability to penetrate human exteriors and get to the bottom of things. The information the detective obtains is not empowering but humbling, as his investigation reveals just how little he can know and how little he can accomplish. A consistent feature of hard-boiled fiction and film noir is that the detective is always initially mistaken about what he thinks he knows. His search is invariably marked by false steps, missteps, detours, wrong turns, and blind alleys. He may eventually figure out what is really going on, but this usually happens far too late for him to bring about a desirable outcome. The noir investigator may solve the case, but the costs to him and others usually outweigh the benefits, and he is often left alone, more cynical, and alienated. He may capture the guilty parties, but the structures of crime and corruption remain intact, bringing a sense of impotence and futility to his activity. The special meaning the detective attaches to his search for knowledge only increases the disappointment of his failure. The detective's investigation does not unlock the door to the security of objective and certain truth but reveals the elusiveness, uncertainty, and insignificance of life.

The private detective is distinguished from amateur investigators like Vincent Parry, who desperately searches for evidence to clear him, because he is not initially emotionally involved in the case. He takes assignments for money to earn his living, but the pay is hardly compensatory given the difficulty and danger of the work and the skills required. The job provides a level of autonomy absent from the employment opportunities available to most working-class men, but the private eye is also dependent upon an unsteady flow of clients. Detectives like Agatha Christie's Hercules Poirot needed only a few scraps of physical evidence and their prodigious powers of deductive reasoning to determine the killer. Suspects were sometimes conveniently gathered under the same roof. The noir detective's efforts are challenged by the subjectivity of truth, the limits of empiricism, and the opaqueness of others. He persists because he is a professional investigator motivated to uncover the truth by the very obstacles to knowledge he encounters in the noir world.

In *Murder, My Sweet* (1944), Jules Amthor tells Marlowe, "I've always credited the private detective with a high degree of omniscience." The private detective would indeed need such power to overcome the subjectivity of truth, the limitations of radical empiricism, and the opaqueness of others. Unable to surmount these difficulties, he sniffs around, asks questions, and stirs up trouble. Before long, someone emerges from the shadows to warn him, bribe him, work him over, or slit his nostril, and he can trace the guilty parties through their hired thugs. Once he is threatened or attacked, the case becomes personal, and his dogged defiance is a badge of honor. The private detective investigates by placing himself at risk, because, given the epistemological limitations of the noir world, there are no other paths to the truth.

Amthor may have been misled by the private detective's smarter-than-thou attitude. The assured demeanor and wisecracking delivery are products of a career spent going through other people's dirty laundry. The detective is confident that there is little that he has not seen and even less that he cannot discover, especially if he suspects the worst. But the epistemological obstacles of the noir world delay his ability to uncover the truth and adversely affect his ability to transform his knowledge into effective action. Gittes' experience in *Chinatown* combines those of his predecessors from the original noir cycle. His initial investigation leads to a dead end, and the truth contains more depravity than even the jaded detective anticipated. The innocent are destroyed, and the force of evil remains free. The private detective's narrative would be a simple story of failure, if, as a professional investigator, he were unable to uncover the truth and solve the case. The fact is that he does uncover the truth; he eventually identifies the culprits. The private detective's narrative is one of hopelessness and despair because he does uncover the truth but finally realizes that knowledge is not efficacious.

ENDNOTES

1. Except for the very brief scene in which Miles Archer is shot.
2. This attempt to describe differs from the approach used by most academic phenomenology, which attempts to describe *universal* experience.
3. The protagonist's first name was changed to Ed in the 1942 film noir.
4. The phrase is spoken in the film version, though only the novel contains the final scene with Iva Archer.

CHAPTER 3

THE EXISTENTIAL
ETHICS OF NOIR

"Don't be too sure I'm as crooked as I'm supposed to be."
—Sam Spade in Hammett's *The Maltese Falcon* (583)

In Plato's *The Republic*, Socrates challenges Thrasymachus' claim that
the life of the unjust is more "profitable"[1] than the life of the just. Socrates
asserts that a fair comparison between the just and unjust requires that
they be examined in their perfect states. It is possible for an unjust man
to be unenlightened about his best interest and act against that interest. In
such cases, injustice would not be profitable, but such ignorance would
not prove the case against injustice. The just person must be perfectly
just; the unjust person must be perfectly unjust. Socrates claims that the
just attempt to get the better of the unjust but do not attempt to get the
better of the just, but the unjust attempt to get the better of the unjust as
well as the just. Therefore, the unjust are required to regard all persons
as enemies. Socrates argues that any group of unjust members will fail

to accomplish its objectives because their efforts will be undermined by "factions, hatred and quarrels among themselves" (Plato, *Republic* 351d).

According to Socrates' usage, a perfectly unjust man is always unjust, in all situations with all persons. If the unjust person is sometimes just, that person admits that sometimes justice is more profitable and undermines Thrasymachus' argument that injustice is always more profitable. Thrasymachus was unwise to allow this definition and could have argued that perfect injustice is the intelligent selective use of unjust practices. Socrates' argument requires this notion of perfect injustice because it eliminates this judicious approach. Socrates acknowledges that a group of robbers "could never have restrained themselves with one another if they were completely unjust, but it is plain that there was a certain justice in them which caused them at least not to do injustice to one another at the same time that they were seeking to do it to others" (Plato, *Republic* 352c). Socrates' statement suggests that people can be what he calls "half bad from injustice," but his (or Plato's) comprehensive view of virtue will not permit this distinction. Socrates does not accept that a person can actually be just, or only "half bad," while engaging in unjust activity (Plato, *Republic* 352c). By his account of virtue, a group of robbers would not be considered unjust about the robbery, yet just because they treated each other fairly during its execution.

The argument about robbers and perfect injustice is a bit of a digression for Socrates, who returns to his main objective, which is to define justice, but this portion of the conversation between Socrates and his interlocutors raises the issue of whether there can be honor among thieves, whether criminals can be principled, and whether virtues are absolute standards relative to circumstances or whether they are matters of degree.

In *The Republic*, Socrates describes his *ideal* state, which is governed by the philosopher-king, who assumes leadership based on his knowledge of the form of the Good. Citizens are assigned to classes within the state based on their aptitudes as determined by the authorities. Though the guardians are held in higher regard, working-class citizens need not fear their leaders. According to Socrates, the true ruler rules for the sake of the ruled in the manner that the true shepherd looks after the best interest of the sheep. The rulers do not exploit members of other classes. In fact, they shun material wealth, leaving that to the workers. Justice prevails when all citizens properly observe and maintain class boundaries. The ideal state is a paradise in which citizens are content to perform duties commensurate with their talents and abilities and receive compensation relative to their natures. The guardians and soldiers achieve the honor and glory they desire and deserve; the workers earn the material rewards they want.

Thrasymachus, on the other hand, describes the state as it *exists*, which is governed by the ruler who has likely seized power and cannot be challenged except by force. Citizens are assigned to classes within the state based on their social, political, and economic status. The ruler rules for his own sake, like a shepherd who tends the flock with the intent to have it slaughtered for profit. The ruling class is about the business of maintaining its own wealth, privilege, and power. The lower classes exist to serve the ruling class and are often left to fend for themselves. Members of the bottom class have every reason to fear their leaders because these leaders have authority over them and have only self-interested concern for their welfare. Thrasymachus' state, the existing state, is a corrupt, hierarchical order in which the few benefit at the expense of the many.

It can be argued that Thrasymachus' definition of justice, that it is "the interest of the stronger,"[2] is not a defense of injustice at all but a realistic appraisal of the state and a charge that what is called justice is actually a betrayal of the state's weaker inhabitants (Plato, *Republic* 338c). Since justice is the interest of the stronger, rulers rule for their own sake, often to the detriment of the ruled. Evidently, Thrasymachus meant to demonstrate that injustice is more profitable than justice to explain why the stronger conduct and perpetuate unjust practices. In Socrates' ideal state, the citizen's virtue is measured by his or her obedience to presumably just laws and customs. In a corrupt society, the relation between the virtue of a member and the laws of the state is strained, if not shattered. The corrupt state does not have the moral authority to dictate ethical standards. Its standards will reflect the interests of the powerful or will be hollow platitudes intended to lend the appearance of morality. Individuals who resist the standards of a corrupt society may be branded criminals, but because the state is unqualified to judge the virtue of a member, some alternative means for judgment are required or will be developed.

In his essay, "The Simple Art of Murder," Raymond Chandler challenges mystery writers of his era to present a more realistic depiction of the society in which their characters operate than that offered by Golden Age authors like Agatha Christie and Ellery Queen. Chandler wanted criminal activity and the detective's investigation moved from the drawing room to the back alley, or to wherever else it most frequently occurs, but he also called for writers to accurately exhibit the social, economic, and political corruption that produces and supports criminal activity. In the following extended passage from "The Simple Art of Murder," Chandler describes the world that the responsible mystery writer must present to be realistic and credible:

> The realist in murder writes of a world in which gangsters can rule nations and almost rule cities, in which hotels and apartment houses and celebrated restaurants are owned by men who made their money out of brothels, in which a screen star can be the finger man for a mob, and the nice man down the hall is a boss of the numbers racket; a world where a judge with a cellar full of bootleg liquor can send a man to jail for having a pint in his pocket, where the mayor of your town may have condoned a murder as an instrument of money-making, where no man can walk down a dark street in safety because law and order are things we talk about but refrain from practicing; a world where you may witness a holdup in broad daylight and see who did it, but you will fade quickly into the crowd rather than tell anyone, because the holdup men may have friends with long guns, or the police may not like your testimony, and in any case the shyster for the defense will be allowed to abuse and vilify you in open court, before a jury of selected morons, without any but the most perfunctory interference from a political judge. (991)

Chandler charges that this is "the world you live in," the existing world. The realism he calls for is not merely the criticism of the criminal but is an indictment of a society permeated with corruption and hypocrisy at the highest levels.

Black Mask editor Joseph T. Shaw, for whom Chandler wrote his early short stories, describes his working-class readers as "hating unfairness, trickery, injustice, cowardly underhandedness; standing for a square deal and a fair show in little or big things," and most of all, "always pulling for the right guy to come out on top" (qtd. in MacShane 46). These are the standards Shaw's readers used to evaluate the virtues of hard-boiled fiction protagonists. The character who upholds these values earns the respect of readers even if that character occasionally operates outside the law or is a career criminal, for the reader's reverence for law and order is undermined in a corrupt society. The reader accepts Thrasymachus' view and applies it to contemporary conditions. The contrast of the standards of the reader and the world summarized by Chandler and offered in the pages of noir fiction, emphasizes the betrayal of so-called *American values*. Shaw's working-class readers support fairness and justice, but hard-boiled characters are surrounded by dishonesty, depravity, and decadence. The right guy rarely comes out on top and is lucky to survive. It is indicative of the corruption of the noir world that working-class protagonists who are accidentally entangled in crime, a frequent noir circumstance, never go to the police. As poor men, they believe they are perceived guilty until miraculously proven innocent. Just as Thrasymachus defined justice from the perspective of the weak, noir fiction and films present what can be called a *gutter's eye view* of the United States, the nightmarish reality of the American Dream as experienced by some of its more marginalized citizens.

I will give considerable attention to the issue of honor among thieves, but the problem of ethics in the noir world is symbolized not by the criminal but by the private detective. The criminal is an outlaw who, by definition, challenges and rejects the authority of the law and the state. He may feel justified in doing so, but his critique comes from one who has chosen to be an outsider. The private detective, on the other hand, is a licensed agent of the law, ostensibly an insider, who finds it impossible to practice his profession with respect for the law and the approved standards of ethical conduct.

Race Williams, perhaps the first noir detective, immediately expresses his attitude concerning ethics when he remarks in the opening pages of Carroll John Daly's *Snarl of the Beast* (1927), "right and wrong are not written on the statutes for me, nor do I find my code of morals in the essays of long-winded professors. My ethics are my own. I'm not saying they're good and I'm not admitting they're bad, and what's more I'm not interested in the opinions of others on the subject" (1). Dashiell Hammett's nameless pre-Spade detective, known simply as the Continental Op, explains in *Red Harvest* (1929) why no external authority, in this case, his employer, can dictate his conduct. "It's right enough for the Agency to have rules and regulations," he begins, "but when you're out on a job you've got to do it the best way you can. And anybody that brings any ethics to Poisonville is going to get them all rusty" (103). Poisonville is officially named Personville. The corruption of the name conveys the corruption of persons and places in hard-boiled America. The private detective is not ethical to the extent that ethics are defined as a set of established rules and standards of conduct, and he regards those who are as naïve and foolish. The detective obeys his own personal code, which he rarely, if ever, explains to others, but which can be inferred from the line he draws to separate himself from those he despises.

The intended consumers of hard-boiled fiction, whom Shaw describes as "hating unfairness, trickery, injustice, cowardly underhandedness; standing for a square deal and a fair show in little or big things," and most of all, "always pulling for the right guy to come out on top," somehow identified with these detectives who registered disdain for conventional morality but adhered to personal standards of integrity. The noir detective is presented as a member of the working-class, whose lonely struggle is to make an honest dollar in a dishonest world. His cynicism and low regard for ethical rules are conditioned by the contradiction between the nation's expressed principles and the existing reality in which pursuit of material gain supersedes all other values. In hard-boiled fiction and film noir, the trail generally leads from working-class subordinates involved in petty crime to the rich and powerful who veil their activities behind a cloak of respectability. The hard-boiled detective may solve the case, that is, he may discover whodunit, but he cannot stop the deterministic forces that operate behind the scenes. The police, politicians, and judges Chandler describes in "The Simple Art of Murder" are responsible for maintaining law and order, but oversee much of the evil-doing to ensure that the profits flow into the proper hands. This is not to say that the working-class is by definition more virtuous than the rich and powerful, but the former has limited access to large-scale crime, while the latter has such entry, coupled with the ability to manipulate the forces of law and order to protect themselves and their ill-gotten gain.

It is the noir detective's determination to uphold those working-class values that Shaw describes, in the face of extensive corruption, that earns the respect of hard-boiled readers. Pulp fiction enthusiasts recognize that the private eye cannot practice conventional ethics in the contingent and corrupt noir world. The hard-boiled detective believes in justice and fairness but not as abstract concepts. He practices these virtues in particular situations with specific individuals who demonstrate that they deserve these considerations. In a world in which ethics are impossible, self-determined personal integrity is all that remains. The private eye's rare confessions of failure are not apologies for transgressions against convention standards of morality or the structures that create, support, and enforce such standards. The detective confesses that he is guilty of betraying his own personal principles, and the offense is greater than disobedience to the law or standards of an abstract morality or corrupt society because the detective has violated the rules he has freely created for himself and therefore has no defense for his unacceptable conduct.

Because the noir world is mostly inhabited by the deceitful and duplicitous, the hard-boiled detective is permitted some latitude in his conduct. To maintain his strategic advantage over his opponents, he must sometimes appear capable of using many of their tactics, but he will not betray the standards Shaw describes. In *The Maltese Falcon*, when Spade weighs the options of sending Brigid over, she asks whether the scales might be balanced in her favor if he had received his anticipated fee for the falcon. Spade snarls, "Don't be too sure I'm as crooked as I'm supposed to be. That sort of reputation might be good business, bringing in high-priced jobs and making it easier to deal with the enemy" (583). Spade is disgusted that Brigid would compare his ends and means to hers. Spade has not been ethical, but he has been dealing with a nest of vipers, and his methods for outmaneuvering his adversaries do not include thievery or murder. He has usually attempted to appear more dishonest than he really is, and it is indicative of the corruption of the noir world that this approach is required to persuade his shady clients to trust him.

The Maltese Falcon, which helped set the standard for film noir, establishes an atmosphere in which the relentless pursuit of material gain results in a world that is irreparably damaged. Each of the principle characters is unscrupulous, and secondary characters are victims or insignificant spectators. Law and order, in the form of the police and district attorney, are mostly irrelevant, if they appear at all. Plenty of films show greedy characters in corrupt surroundings, but Huston succeeds in establishing the noir world as *the* world, "the world you live in." Most of the film is shot in interiors, creating a claustrophobic atmosphere and the impression that nothing exists beyond those walls. Characters are photographed in cramped spaces, at close angles that reduce or eliminate space around them.

The characters are the most significant contributors to the corrupt atmosphere. Brigid O'Shaunessey is duplicitous; her only redeeming quality is the transparency of much of her deceitfulness. Joel Cairo is soft-spoken and polite but always game for a double-cross. Caspar Gutman is jocular, but deadly, with a henchman at the ready. Wilmer's tics and twitches betray his psychosis. These adversaries are defined by their willingness to do whatever is necessary to acquire the falcon and thereby establish their world through their presence because in this tale, there are no good characters. None of the principles operates from an ethical base but adapts strategy to the occasion. Joel Cairo first attempts to search Spade's office at gunpoint. When that fails, he adjusts his approach and arranges to avail himself of Spade's investigative services.

Cairo confesses his indifference to the law as he hires Spade to find the falcon. Spade asks, "You're not hiring to commit any murders or burglaries, but to get it back, if possible, in an honest, lawful way?" Cairo replies, "If possible, but, in any case, with discretion." Gutman initally refuses Spade's suggestion that Wilmer be offered as the "fall guy," responding, "I feel toward Wilmer here, exactly as if he were my own son." But once Wilmer's surrender to the authorities becomes a necessary condition for receiving the falcon, Gutman reveals, in practical terms, that surrogate fatherhood is subordinate to material wealth. "Well, Wilmer," Gutman apologizes, "I'm sorry indeed to lose you, but I want you to know I couldn't be fonder of you if you were my own son. But, well, if you lose a son, it's possible to get another. There's only one Maltese falcon."

The depiction of the noir world as irredeemably fallen is completed by the ambiguous morality of Sam Spade. In the prenoir detective movie, crime appeared as an aberration, and criminals were an interruption of a stable, just society. Once the case was solved and the perpetrators were arrested or killed, order was restored. In a world in which the core is rotten, where law and fatherhood, if they exist at all, are at the service of the relentless pursuit of material gain, there can be no justice, and one is foolish to practice conventional ethics.

Spade's questionable tactics are accepted by the viewer because it becomes clear, despite his hard-boiled appearance of indifference, that he is involved with unprincipled clients. His line to Brigid, "Don't be too sure I'm as crooked as I'm supposed to be," indicates that some of Spade's behavior is an act intended to keep his adversaries off balance. Spade is not ethical, but he has a personal code, a line he will not cross, that distinguishes him from those willing to murder to get their hands on the falcon. Spade's code is not explicitly expressed but is implied during his second meeting with Gutman. When Gutman asks Spade if he knows what "the bird" is, Spade first answers, "Oh, I know what it's supposed to look like." He then looks sternly into Gutman's eyes and says, "And I know the value in human life you people put on it." The pursuit of material wealth, to be gained at any cost, including human sacrifice, results in a cesspool society. The audience, the part of it that identifies with Spade, shares his contempt for the conspirators and a world built upon greed, corruption, and hypocrisy.

In his essay "The Simple Art of Murder," Chandler describes the qualities of the honorable detective in terms that resemble Joseph T. Shaw's working-class readers. The hard-boiled private eye, Chandler explains,

> is a relatively poor man or he would not be a detective at all. He is a common man or he could not go among common people. He has a sense of character, or he would not know his job. He will take no man's money dishonestly and no man's insolence without a due and dispassionate revenge. (992)

Chandler tells us that the detective is most of all a man of honor "by instinct," which means his personal code of conduct "is not found in the long-winded essays of professors," and he does not need or want ethical instruction. Ethical rules are needed by those who do not instinctively know the difference between right and wrong.

In Chandler's first novel, *The Big Sleep* (1939), Private Eye Philip Marlowe is hired by General Sternwood to handle a case of blackmail involving the General's daughter, Carmen. Before the day is over, the trail leads to a pornography ring, two missing persons, and two homicides. The blackmailers have pornographic photographs of Carmen. Vivian Regan, the General's older daughter, has a missing husband, and Eddie Mars, a gambler, has a missing wife. Rumor is that Vivian's husband and Eddie Mar's wife are hiding out together. The pornographic dealer, Arthur Gwynn Geiger, is soon found murdered, as is the Sternwood's chauffeur, who tried to intervene on Carmen's behalf. The blackmailer, Joe Brody, appropriates Geiger's inventory of pornographic material and is soon shot and killed by Geiger's lover and assistant. This bewildering array of events is not out of the ordinary in Chandler's corrupt, realistic world of hard-boiled fiction.

An early passage in Marlowe's office establishes the detective as a working-class supporter of the square deal. When Brody is killed, the blackmail case is officially settled, and the next day, Vivian Regan arrives with a check for Marlowe's services. When she notices the dingy condition of his professional space, Vivian says, "You don't put up much of a front," and Marlowe replies, "You can't make much money in this trade, if you're honest" (Chandler, *Big Sleep* 630). Though the blackmail case is settled, Marlowe is concerned that General Sternwood's unexpressed wish is that he finds Vivian's missing husband, Rusty Regan, who was also his friend. Though he has been well paid, Marlowe feels responsible to complete the unfinished business for the aged General, whom he has come to respect for his lack of hypocrisy.

Marlowe's advocacy of the fair show and the right guy coming out on top is best demonstrated by his experience with Harry Jones. Though the diminutive grifter is described by Marlowe's narration as a "small man in a big man's world," he conducts his affairs with integrity (Chandler, *Big Sleep* 716). The poor person has more reason to feel justified in being dishonest and deserves more respect when he is not. Jones has fallen on hard times since the "big boys" pushed his bookie boss out of town, taking over the operation. Jones' modest economic status is displayed by his tattered, out-of-date clothing. Marlowe conveys Jones' condition in empirical fashion, telling us that the grifter "wore a double-breasted dark gray suit that was too wide in the shoulders and had too much lapel. Over this, open, an Irish tweed coat with some badly worn spots. A lot of foulard tie bulged out and was rainspotted across his lapels" (Chandler, *Big Sleep* 711). Jones has information to sell concerning the whereabouts of the missing Mr. Regan and Mrs. Mars. When Marlowe mentions going to the police, Jones admonishes him. "I haven't pulled anything in here," he said steadily. "I come in talking two Cs. That's still the price. I come because I thought I'd get a take it or leave it, one right gee to another. Now you're waving cops at me. You oughta be ashamed of yourself" (Chandler, *Big Sleep* 716).

Jones' sense of honor catches Marlowe off guard, but he recovers, concedes the point, and agrees to Jones' terms. As the grifter explains how he knows what he knows, Marlowe grows impressed with Jones and remarks to himself that "the little man wasn't so dumb after all. A three for a quarter grifter wouldn't even think such thoughts, let alone know how to express them" (Chandler, *Big Sleep* 714). In the hard-boiled world, occupation and socioeconomic status are not indicators of a man's intelligence or integrity.

Jones is acting on behalf of Agnes Lozelle, former girlfriend and partner of the dearly departed Joe Brody. "It's not so easy for a dame to get by these days," Jones explains (Chandler, *Big Sleep* 713). Marlowe is aware that Agnes is playing Jones for a sap, but he still admires the little man's loyalty. Marlowe (unarmed) is later forced to stand by in another room as Jones, at gunpoint, is ordered to divulge Agnes' whereabouts. Jones gives the thug false information that is believed, but he is compelled to swallow poison nevertheless. Marlowe tells the dead Jones, "You lied to him and drank your cyanide like a little gentleman. You died like a poisoned rat, Harry, but you're no rat to me" (Chandler, *Big Sleep* 723). Agnes did not care about Jones, though he died protecting her, and complained that *she* "got a raw deal." Though several people are killed during the case, Jones is the only character whose death is openly lamented by Marlowe. Jones was a "right gee" who practiced the square deal and deserved better.

Chandler describes the private detective as a man of honor "by instinct," and hard-boiled fiction readers and film noir viewers are permitted and expected to trust their instincts and standards to determine which characters they will regard as honorable. The existential ethics of noir offers no abstract moral theory. There is no template to tell readers and viewers which character is a "right gee" and which is not. Ethical standards speak in terms of black and white and imply that we can clearly distinguish between good and bad, right and wrong. The French word *noir* literally translates as *black*, but the noir world exists in shades of gray that convey ambiguity. In a world in which "hotels and apartment houses and celebrated restaurants are owned by men who made their money out of brothel, in which a screen star might be a finger man for a mob, and the nice man down the hall is a boss of the numbers racket," people are seldom what they seem to be. In Chandler's novel, Marlowe's narration shares the detective's revised impressions of Harry Jones, but in Howard Hawks' film version of *The Big Sleep* (1946), there is no voiceover narration, and the viewer is not led to a specific moral judgment. If the viewer feels that Jones received a "tough break," it is because the viewer has decided that the grifter, despite his criminal status, has earned and deserves respect.

The move toward the treatment of movie crime characters as worthy of moral evaluation rather than reactionary condemnation actually occurs during the late period of the gangster cycle of Hollywood films that predates film noir. Two early gangster films, *Little Caesar* (1930) and *The Public Enemy* (1931), begin with warnings to the audience about the growing infestation of criminals in our ghettos and sound the alarm that they must be exterminated like insects or rodents. Each film ends with the violent death of the protagonist at the hands of the law or his enemies, reinforcing the standard that crime does not pay. At the end of the decade, the popular actor James Cagney, who starred in *The Public Enemy*, would appear in two films that present a different take on the gangster.

In the first and more famous of the two, *Angels with Dirty Faces* (1938), Cagney plays Rocky Sullivan, an amiable but dangerous criminal who returns to his old slum neighborhood to settle a score. As he engages in criminal activity, Rocky also helps his boyhood friend, now a priest, keep an admiring group of delinquent boys out of serious trouble. Towards the end of the film, Father Jerry Connelly wages a crusade to expose crime and corruption, and when the priest's life is threatened, Rocky comes to his aid, killing members of his own gang. Rocky is eventually captured, tried, and sentenced to die in the electric chair, but he voluntarily provides evidence and testimony that leads to other convictions. In the film's final scene, Connelly visits death row and asks Rocky for one last favor, one that requires courage. Not the "courage of heroics or bravado," Connelly clarifies, "but the kind only you and I and God know about." Connelly wants Rocky to pretend to die "yellow" so the neighborhood boys, and millions like them, will not honor his memory. If he agrees to Connelly's request, he will forever be remembered as a coward. Rocky adamantly refuses, but when he reaches the electric chair, he screams for mercy as Connelly whispers a prayer.

Rocky Sullivan is problematic for those who adhere to strict notions of morality. Rocky is a hardened criminal and a ruthless killer, but he is motivated by friendship and his personal sense of justice to support Connelly's efforts on behalf of the poor and defenseless. Rocky also sacrifices his pride, "the only thing I got left," he says, for the benefit of the underprivileged boys. How are we to judge him? Connelly's prayer implies that Rocky is worthy of God's forgiveness, and therefore ours too. Rocky's final acts are honorable, and perhaps these cannot erase a lifetime of crime, but our visceral response suggests that his courage cannot simply be denied or disregarded. *Angels with Dirty Faces* was enormously popular with moviegoers, and the following year, Warner Brothers released *The Roaring Twenties* (1939), starring Cagney as another gangster who finally opposes organized crime.

The year 1940 was a transitional one from the gangster cycle to the film noir cycle. Film noir, as much as any movie genre or cycle, helped solidify the role of the antihero. Strictly speaking, the antihero is a character that lacks traditional heroic qualities such as idealism and courage and is consequently at odds with the society that glorifies those traits. The film noir antihero undermines this definition and relation. Cagney's gangsters achieve honorable status as they finally join society's efforts to fight crime and corruption. Criminal antiheroes of the film noir period remain committed to the criminal world against society but are still perceived as honorable. The film noir antihero is generally a brooding, cynical loner with ambiguous morals, alienated from a society perceived as thoroughly corrupt. Though his criminal status implies that he is dishonorable, his honorable actions serve as a contrasting commentary on the polluted world he inhabits.

In *High Sierra* (1940), Roy Earle embodies a certain heroic dimension that survives despite the fact that he is shot and killed by the authorities, or perhaps because he is gunned down, at the end of the film. During the movie, Earle befriends a rural family and extricates them from liability for an automobile accident. He falls for a crippled young woman among them and pays for an operation to mend her club foot, only to be rejected by her once she recovers and can "have fun." Earle shelters the battered

Marie, who falls in love with him, and honestly tells her that he cannot return her feelings. He refuses to double-cross his dead gang boss and shoots a cop turned crook who tries. As the police nets encircle Earle, he puts Marie on a bus to safety and literally heads for the hills. He finally exposes himself to gunfire when he realizes Marie is in custody at the base of his mountain refuge. Throughout the film, Earle is presented as a ruthless criminal who is somehow also a man of principle. Earle is nick-named "Mad Dog" by the press, but he has been anything but a mad dog. In fact, his affection for a little dog that he and Marie adopt and cannot bear to leave behind contributes to his death.

Earle, an aging outlaw, appears as a man of integrity, a member of a dying breed, who is consequently out of step with the corrupt world he must engage. Big Mac, his partner in crime from the old days, forced to deal with modern men of dishonor, tells Earle, "It's a relief just talkin' to a guy like you." The film begins with Earle's release from prison, and he is so uncertain about the nature of a changing world that he tells the driver to take him to the park so he can make sure that "grass is still green and trees are still growing." Pa, the rural farmer Earle assists, represents a more honorable era. He refers to himself and Earle as "oldtimers" and calls Earle "our kind," implying that they share old-fashioned principles that are rapidly disappearing. When Earle is forced to flee, he heads away from the corruption of the modern city to the timeless freedom symbolized by the mountains and open space. Another oldtimer tells Earle that the gangster seems to be "rushing towards death." No longer able to exist peacefully in a degenerate world, Earle retreats to a mountain from which there is no escape, except through death. His extinction symbolizes the passing of an old order and his escape from the new. Earle's departure is referred to as a "crash out," the term used by convicts to describe a prison break. In the film's last frame, after Earle is shot and killed, a tearful Marie looks toward the sky and softly cries "He's free."

The viewer can sympathize with Earle's attempt to find a place for himself in the world and also with his feelings about his society's rejection of him. Despite his criminal status, Earle appears to have domestic ambitions. On his way to his assignment, he stops at the Indiana farm his family once owned and offers a boy tips on where to catch the big fish. He takes Marie as a common-law wife, and they adopt a little dog named Pard. One can imagine that if Earle had received his payment for the fenced loot, he would have changed his name, bought another farm, and settled down.

Another film that appeared early in the cycle offers a criminal character even more troublesome for moralists than Roy Earle. This protagonist is without known ties to anyone or anyplace and is determined to remain an outsider.

This Gun for Hire (1942) features Philip Raven, a stoical professional assassin. Raven is hired by Willard Gates to kill an informant. Gates pays Raven with marked stolen bills and then reports the murder, and Raven's involvement, to the police. When Raven discovers he has been double-crossed, he goes after Gates. Unbeknownst to Raven, Gates is an agent of Alvin Brewster, who runs a chemical company that is selling a secret formula for poisonous gas to the Nazis. Raven learns this information from Ellen Graham, a singer in Gates' nightclub who is secretly helping federal authorities. Fearful that Raven will succeed in killing Gates before she can get the evidence, Ellen tries to persuade Raven to help her obtain a confession. "This war is everybody's business," she says. Raven is unconcerned about Gates' treasonous activities and is unmoved by Ellen's patriotic appeal. He has only one thing on his mind: revenge. At the end of the film, though, Raven beats the police and federal authorities to Gates and gets the confession before killing him.

Raven's decisions and actions are problematic for ethics. One might argue that the informant he kills was not innocent, but Raven also kills the informant's secretary/mistress because she just happens to be there and witnesses the murder. In fact, Raven is preparing to shoot Ellen in an abandoned building when he is distracted by approaching people, and she scurries away. When Raven finally agrees to get the confession from Gates, he consents for personal reasons. Raven is surrounded by police and needs Ellen's help to escape, so he makes a deal to get the evidence in return for her assistance. During the time they are hiding,

Ellen is compassionate and tender with Raven, something he has not experienced. Her interest is not romantic: The police detective pursuing Raven, Michael Crane, is her fiancé. Raven develops enough trust in Ellen to share nightmarish memories of beatings at the hands of a vicious aunt and reform school authorities. Later in the film, Raven arrives at Gates' house in time to interrupt an attempt on Ellen's life. She is not completely comfortable with him, but Raven assures her. "Look, I'm not going to hurt you," he says, "You treated me okay." When Raven finally confronts Gates, the latter signs the confession at gunpoint and begs for mercy. Gates blames the entire affair on Brewster, not understanding that Raven is uninterested in the espionage. Raven snaps, "You tried to kill that girl. That girl is my friend." Raven foils the treasonous plans of Gates and Brewster, but one might contend that his reasons and actions are not ethical.

Raven does not do the right thing for the right reason, but by the end of the film, he is regarded as a hero, or an antihero, because, like Earle, he acted in accordance with the standards Shaw describes. Raven is shown to be a remorseless killer, bent on revenge. He does not care about the law or the sale of the secret formula to the Nazis, but he subordinates his thirst for vengeance out of respect for the principles of friendship, honor, and loyalty in this concrete situation with Ellen Graham. The "unfairness, trickery, injustice, [and] cowardly underhandedness," hated by Shaw's readers is characterized by Gates, who hires Raven, then double-crosses him, and then evades responsibility for his acts by blaming Brewster. Ellen makes a deal with Raven and keeps her commitment, even though she must withhold evidence from her detective fiancé. Ellen represents the working-class values of the "square deal" and "fair show."

Raven honors their agreement and his commitment to working-class values by making the ultimate sacrifice. Crane reaches the scene at Nitro Chemical just after Raven shoots Gates. Crane only knows that Raven is a professional killer; Raven knows that Crane is a cop who is also Ellen's fiancé. Raven has the opportunity to kill Crane but does not and is fatally wounded by Crane. The dying Raven hands Ellen the confession and asks, "Did I do all right for you?" Ellen answers that he did. Ellen Graham embodies the qualities of the conventional heroine. She is engaged to a police officer and helps the federal authorities for the right reasons. And in her judgment, Raven did all right.

The protagonists examined thus far are typical of those found in the world of film noir. They are not ethical, but they resolve the problem of ethical engagement with others in a corrupt world by remaining loners. Raven shuns associations with other people, reserving his affection and admiration for stray cats. "They're on their own," he says, "They don't need anybody." In *He Walked by Night* (1949), thief-turned-killer Roy Martin works alone and lives alone, with only a small dog for companionship. Phyllis Dietrichson envies Walter Neff's solitary personal space in *Double Indemnity*. "It sounds wonderful," she tells him, "Just strangers besides you. You don't know them. You don't hate them." Loner criminals resemble private detectives in their determination to keep company with the only people they trust: themselves.

Socrates claims that gang members involved in unjust enterprises cannot succeed because of "factions, hatred, and quarrels among themselves," and in film noir, there is evidence, some bordering on the absurd, to support his position. In *Criss Cross*, Steve Thompson joins forces with Slim Dundee's gang to rob an armored car with the agreement that the elderly driver, Pop, will not be harmed. During the robbery, Dundee shoots Pop, Thompson attacks Dundee, a shootout ensues among the criminals, and only half the loot is stolen. In *White Heat* (1949) "Big Ed" Somers challenges Cody Jarrett's position as top man in the gang. While Jarrett is in prison, Big Ed kills Jarrett's mother and is joined by Jarrett's wife. Jarrett escapes jail, kills Big Ed, and reclaims his wife. In *Odds Against Tomorrow* (1959), Johnny Ingram and Earl Slater reluctantly partner to rob a bank and then turn against each other during the robbery. Slater is a white bigot; Ingram, a black man, is distrustful of most whites. While they argue over the keys to the getaway car, the police arrive and Ingram and Slater flee on foot, shooting at each other. They chase each other to the tops of oil storage tanks. Shots are fired, the tanks explode, and the blast kills them both. There is certainly a good deal of dishonor among thieves in the world of film noir, but the issue is whether there can be honor among them.

The question of honor among thieves, as it is usually put, reduces the human characters involved to the concept of thief. A thief is a person who steals. Stealing is a dishonorable practice, so a person who steals is dishonorable. A group of thieves consists of several dishonorable persons. Because thieves are by definition dishonorable, there can be no honor among thieves. This approach is attractive because it provides a means to simplify the complexity of moral judgment. The existential ethics of noir rejects such attempts to reduce persons or principles to concepts. As was observed in the existential epistemology of noir, a person's life cannot be reduced, defined, or understood by a few terms. A thief is a person who steals, but a person who steals is not simply a thief but is a person whose actions consist of more than thievery. Seeing people as thieves is a product of a narrow morality intended to make thought about the complexity and ambiguity of human action unnecessary.

The legend of Robin Hood (prince of thieves) offers an example of a person who robs the rich to give to the oppressed poor. If one reduces Robin Hood to thief, then he and his band of men are by definition dishonorable. When Robin Hood's activities on behalf of the poor are included, that simplistic definition is problematic if one judges unlawful actions on behalf of the oppressed poor to be honorable. In a scene from the Warner Brothers screen version, *The Adventures of Robin Hood* (1938), Robin and his Saxon men waylay Sir Guy's convoy and capture a huge sum of loot. Marian has reduced Robin's band to thieves, and at the feast, she sarcastically remarks about their plans for the plunder. Upon hearing her charge, Robin leaps onto the table and asks his men, "What shall we do with these riches? Divide it among ourselves?" "No!" they vehemently shout, "This money is for King Richard!"[3] A little later, Robin leads Marian away from the celebration to those who have been beaten and tortured by the Normans and asks if they have had enough to eat. "God bless you, Robin," a battered elderly woman says. Marian concedes that her judgment may have been hasty.

The answer to the question of whether there can be honor among thieves is that it depends on whether the thieves themselves are honorable, that is to say, the issue is not about the relatively simple concept of the thief but is about the complex actions of specific persons. Whether Roy Earle's and Philip Raven's good actions compensate for their crimes, or whether their crimes are justified, is left to the individual viewer to judge. The existential ethics of noir does not divide the world into dishonorable criminals and honorable law-abiding citizens, but it divides the criminal world, "the world you live in," into honorable and dishonorable criminals. Honorable criminals abide by the ethics of noir, dishonorable criminals do not. An "ethical" criminal adheres to the working-class values of integrity, loyalty, friendship, commitment, and professionalism. He is referred to as a "right gee" or "stand-up guy," by other honorable men who are the only judges he cares about. He is the very opposite of the unjust type Socrates describes. His conduct does not facilitate "factions, hatred and quarrels" but contributes to a successful criminal endeavor.

The divergence between honorable and dishonorable criminals is effectively portrayed in *The Asphalt Jungle* (1950) and is displayed through the themes of friendship and betrayal. *The Asphalt Jungle* is a masterful example of the heist film noir, in which a team of criminals is assembled to plan and execute an intricate robbery. The group's success is dependent upon each member's ability and willingness to perform his individual duties and coordinate his efforts in a cooperative manner. If any member fails to live up to his responsibilities, the team risks a failed mission and each participant risks capture, imprisonment, or death.

The members of the team are selected for their professional talents, but personal qualities of integrity and character ultimately prove to be more important. The distinction between *man* as concept and *a man* as an individual is illustrated in Doc Riedenschneider's evaluation of Dix Handley. The team requires a "boxman" to open the safe, a driver for the getaway car, and a hooligan to handle any rough stuff that might occur. Riedenschneider is unhappy about the need for a hooligan because "most of these fellas are drug addicts. They're a no-good lot. Violence is all they know, but they are, unfortunately, necessary." The hooligan, defined as a mindless thug, is a potential danger to a group that requires reliability, stability, and judgment. When Riedenschneider considers the hooligan as a concept, he has reason to worry.

Doc Riedenschneider meets Dix Handley at Cobby's betting establishment without knowing Handley is a hooligan. Handley wishes to place a bet and is insulted by Cobby's reference to his mounting debt. Handley angrily returns with the $2,300 payment, which he tosses at Cobby, telling him to count it. Riedenschneider watches this scene and later tells an agitated Cobby that perhaps the gambling debt was a matter of honor for Handley. "Him? That hooligan? Honor? Don't make me laugh," Cobby responds. Realizing that the group needs a hooligan, Riedenschneider observes Handley more closely, then requests him as a member of the gang. "He impressed me as a very determined man, and far from stupid," Doc tells the others. Handley, evaluated as an individual, does not match the description of the hooligan Riedenschneider first offered, and to his credit Riedenschneider revises his judgment. As events unfold, Handley is the person Riedenschneider takes into his confidence when he becomes suspicious of Emmerich. "I can talk to you, I think," Doc tells Dix.

Circumstances prove that Riedenschneider was wise to base his assessment on his personal observation of an individual rather than the cold analysis of an abstract concept. After the robbery, Riedenschneider and Handley hide out together and a short-lived friendship based on mutual respect develops between these very different men. Handley often jumps to wrong conclusions, conclusions which allow him to settle matters with violence, but he listens to Riedenschneider's intelligent presentations of alternatives. When Handley wants to kill the double-crossing Emmerich, Riedenschneider calmly explains that death is an easy out for Emmerich, who now has the responsibility of repairing matters. When Handley sees Riedenschneider's photograph in the newspaper in connection with the robbery, he assumes somebody squealed and threatens revenge, but Riedenschneider reasons that if someone had talked, all their pictures would be in the paper. Riedenschneider is a known criminal mastermind recently released from prison. Some cop "with a few brains" put two and two together. When the men separate, Riedenschneider offers Handley $50,000 in robbery loot in exchange for $1,000 spending money. Handley has no use for the jewels and refuses them but provides the cash. Though Handley is the strong-arm man, he comes to admire Riedenschneider's different brand of toughness. Riedenschneider declines Handley's offer of a gun for protection and proceeds through a group of loitering policemen. The bemused Handley calls Riedenschneider a "funny little guy," and adding, "[H]e's got plenty of guts."

The theme of friendship is also presented in the relationship between Dix Handley and Doll Conovan. Dix's face initially registers mild annoyance when Doll arrives at his apartment unannounced, in the middle of the night, carrying a suitcase. Doll soon bursts into tears but does not share her troubles and apologizes for disturbing Dix. Handley is aware that Doll's place of employment, a "clip joint," was raided. "It would have to be on pay night," Doll exclaims. She has been locked out of her apartment and needs a place to stay. It seems that Dix and Doll are former lovers, and Dix is concerned about Doll's desire to renew their affair. Nevertheless, Dix allows her to stay. A few days later, Doll tells Dix that she has found new accommodations. A girlfriend has a temporary job out of town, and the rent at her local apartment is paid until the end of the month. As Doll prepares to depart, she and Dix have the follow exchange:

> DOLL: I can't go living off you forever, can I?
> DIX: [Rising from his chair.] I was glad to help out.
> DOLL: Well, maybe I can do something for you sometime.
> DIX: You don't owe me a thing. How are you fixed for dough?
> DOLL: A couple of bucks. Enough. No [refusing the cash Dix extends.], I'm all through bothering.

Friends come to each other's aid in times of need. The working-class film noir characters realize that any one of them is potentially one payment away from being kicked out into the street. They can take some comfort in knowing that there is someone to whom they can turn. Friends do not take advantage of generosity, realizing that those assisting them have little to spare. Doll takes the amount of help she needs but no more. Dix will not accept that his friend, a human being in trouble, owes him anything. Generosity is a gift voluntarily extended out of caring, not a moral obligation that requires reciprocity. They are no longer lovers, and Dix does not want to resume that relationship, but he still cares about Doll. Near the end of the film, when the wounded Dix is set to make a dangerous drive to Kentucky, Doll will not allow him to travel alone and refuses to tell him where she parked the car unless he agrees to take her along. If Dix and Doll are morally obligated to help each other, their acts would seem more like imposed duties than gifts of kindness. Dix's and Doll's kindness give these scenes their poignancy because neither obeys a requirement, but each treats the other with compassion.

Early in *The Asphalt Jungle*, Gus Minissi expresses his friendly concern for Dix Handley by refusing to return Dix's pistol, which Handley uses to earn a living. "Go ahead, smack me down," Gus tells him. Dix seems hurt and replies, "You know I wouldn't do that." Gus is aware that for good reason, Handley is the prime suspect in a series of petty robberies in the area, and the police are on alert. Handley explains that he cannot "knock off" because he needs $2,300 to pay off his gambling debt to Cobby. "I just can't be in Cobby's debt and keep my self-respect," Dix expresses. "I've got a grand put away," Gus says, "You can have that. I guess I can dig up the rest." Handley is relieved to have support but is somewhat ashamed that he needs it. As the dejected Dix leaves the diner, Gus tells him, "Don't get your flag at half-mast. Remember you still got ol' Gus." Gus understands that Dix would put himself at risk rather than ask for help. Handley's situation is not desperate; he is not being pressured by Cobby for payment, but Gus appreciates that Dix's sense of honor is involved in his need to pay off his debt, and he is willing to "bust a gut" to get the cash to keep his friend out of trouble.

The criminal characters in *The Asphalt Jungle* survive through their network of friends. There is the sense that they are all in the same working-class boat and have only each other in times of trouble.

Gus Minissi turns to Louie Ciavelli to raise the additional money he promised Dix Hanley. Louie at first refuses to help, shouts, "I've got mouths to feed, rent to pay, and all that stuff" at Gus, and hangs up the phone. He drifts into his bedroom, watches his sleeping wife and infant son, and calls Gus back, saying, "I guess I can make it all right." The viewer can imagine Louie considering the possibility that he and his family may need help someday, and he will have only his friends to turn to. Later in the film, when the cops come to arrest Gus, he keeps them at bay long enough to warn Dix and direct him and Riedenschneider to a safe hideout. The sanctuary is owned by Eddie Donato, who lets the fugitives stay out of friendship to Gus.

Several acts of friendship and treachery in *The Asphalt Jungle* involve money. The honorable characters value friendship above money; for the dishonorable, money serves as the catalyst for betrayal. The dishonorable criminals are the money managers, Cobby and Emmerich. Cobby runs a profitable bookie joint but is so nervous about financial transactions that he admits, "[M]oney makes me sweat." The "great" Alonso Emmerich is a wealthy criminal attorney (pun intended) who handles only the biggest cases. His mansion boasts servants, and he has an additional cottage for his young mistress, Angela Phinlay.

Emmerich's need for money exposes the trickery and cowardly underhandedness, disliked by Joseph T. Shaw's readers, at the root of his character. Emmerich's role in the robbery is to provide operating capital and arrange to have the loot fenced after the heist. Despite his high standard of living, Emmerich is actually broke. If he cannot raise the capital for the caper he will forfeit his opportunity to share the profits. Honorable criminals turn to their friends during difficult times; dishonorable criminals attempt to double-cross their partners. Emmerich convinces Cobby to supply the capital and tells the thieves, after the robbery, that he needs more time to secure the money to exchange for the stolen jewels. The loot is to be left with him because the police would not think to search his property.

Riedenschneider recognizes the double-cross and shots are fired, leaving Bob Brannum (Emmerich's partner in the scheme) dead, Handley wounded, and Emmerich pleading for a mercy killing. Handley can hardly comprehend such cowardly underhandedness and shouts at Emmerich, "Are you a man or what? Trying to gyp and double-cross me and with no guts for it. What's inside you? What's keeping you alive?" When the police come to arrest Emmerich, he takes the coward's way out and commits suicide. Riedenschneider explains to Handley that Emmerich's decision was foolish, for he would not have received more than a few years prison time. Handley remarks that Emmerich "even double-crossed himself."

The only friends Cobby and Emmerich have are those they have bought with money, and their relationships provide examples of dishonor among thieves. Cobby places his faith in Lt. Ditrich, the corrupt cop on his payroll, but when Ditrich is pressured from his superior to make an arrest, the only appeal Cobby can make is to offer more money. Ditrich refuses to cooperate, and Cobby threatens to expose him. The angry Ditrich slaps Cobby around until the sobbing bookie pleads for mercy. Cobby does not expose Ditrich but signs a confession incriminating his comrades in the crime. Betrayal is judged the most cowardly act among criminals. It is one thing to be a declared enemy, it is quite another to double-cross one's chosen partners. Emmerich's only trusted associate is his paid detective, Bob Brannum. Brannum has an idea to help Emmerich raise the needed capital but wants to know "What's in it for me?" before he will share. Brannum is both amused and disgusted that Emmerich is reduced to double-crossing his partners. "You big boys. What have you got?" he asks, "Front. Nothing but front." Emmerich, anticipating the robbery money, promised his mistress, Angela, a trip to Cuba. When the police visit the cottage and inform the couple that Emmerich is going to jail, Angela turns to him and with utter sincerity asks him, "What about my trip, Uncle Lon?"

The Killing (1956), the second heist noir masterpiece, makes explicit the working-class economic pressures implied in *The Asphalt Jungle*. In hard-boiled fiction and film noir, the professional criminal is motivated to steal by his unwillingness to submit to the alternative. Crime has its risks, but the probability of imprisonment or death is preferred to the insufferable bondage of legal employment. Noir criminals receive sympathy from working-class readers and audiences that can identify with those who reject wage slavery, also known as "death on the install-ment plan." These criminals do not *earn* more money than their fellow working-class counterparts; in fact, they are usually in worse economic condition, but they retain the autonomy lost to those who sell their labor in the legal free market. Of the honorable criminals in *The Asphalt Jungle*, only Gus Minissi is shown to have a legal source of income: He owns a diner.

In *The Killing*, all the characters, except the protagonist, are working men, and for them, the line between legitimate and illegitimate business is fuzzy. A scene from *Force of Evil* (1949) illustrates the ambiguity, as Leo Morse's wife, Sylvia, begs her husband not to get involved with his gangster brother:

> SYLVIA: Don't have anything to do with him, Leo. You're a businessman.
> LEO: Yes, I've been a businessman all my life and honest I don't know what a business is.
> SYLVIA: Well, you had a garage, you had a real estate business.
> LEO: A lot you know. Real estate business! Living from mortgage to mortgage, stealing credit like a thief. And the garage! That was a business! Three cents overcharge on every gallon of gas; two cents for the chauffeur, and a penny for me. A penny for one thief, two cents for the other.

The working-class man who wishes to operate a small business "hon-est and respectable," as Leo describes his current enterprise, a numbers bank, is faced with feeling like a crook of one sort or another. Given this corruption, working men in film noir can rationalize their decisions to steal.

The Killing involves the planning and implementation of a racetrack robbery. The team, except for the leader, Johnny Clay, consists of men who work at or near the track. Clay, a career felon recently released from prison, explains, "[N]one of these men are criminals in the usual sense of the word. They've all got jobs and they all lead seemingly normal, decent lives. But they've got their share of problems and they've all got a little larceny in them." Mike O'Reilly is a track bartender who hopes to gain money for an operation for his ailing wife. Randy Kennan is a cop in debt over his head to a loan shark. George Peatty is a cuckold teller worried that his voluptuous, avaricious wife will leave him unless he can make a big score. Marvin Unger's motivation is not offered, but he has worked as a bookkeeper for ten years with the same company. Even the professional criminals Clay hires have legitimate sources of income. Maurice Oboukhoff is a chess bum who occasionally earns money wrestling, and Nikki Arane operates a dilapidated rifle range.

The characters in *The Killing* are presented as respectable men who are not stealing in order to live luxuriously but are trying to obtain some relief from financial pressure. The implication is that economic forces will inevitably place working-class men in circumstances that will require them to take extreme chances and break the law. The men bring the same honorable characteristics that they apply in their "normal, decent" lives of legal employment to their roles as amateur criminals. With the exception of Johnny Clay and Marvin Unger, the characters in *The Killing* are not friends, as a few of the robbers were in *The Asphalt Jungle*. The robbery requires even more synchronized timing and teamwork than was needed in the earlier film, but because the characters' relationships are not based on friendship, the honorable quality that will determine success in *The Killing* is professionalism.

During the roundtable planning session, Johnny Clay explains that two men will be hired to perform specific tasks. They will be paid in advance, will not share in the take, and will not know more than their individual roles. The two professional criminals have needed skills not possessed by the other members. Mike O'Reilly wants to know how they can depend upon men who are not equally sharing the risks. The sense of interdependency apparent in *The Asphalt Jungle* seems absent. Clay, a professional criminal himself, responds. "Simple," he says, "These guys are pros. They can't afford to weasel on a deal. If they did they'd be washed up." Criminals who fail to meet their responsibilities risk professional standing and employment opportunities.

Clay's explanation indicates another weakness in Socrates' position, that there cannot be honor among thieves. The criminal has a practical incentive to conduct himself honorably. The allegedly dishonorable criminal who understands self-interest recognizes that "factions, hatred and quarrels" undermine his chances for success as he risks his freedom and his life. A felonious enterprise is dangerous enough without the complications of internal conflict. He can double-cross his mates after the robbery, but unless the money he steals from his partners will last him a lifetime and carry him far enough to escape acts of retribution, he will find himself unable to secure future employment as a member of a team. He will be forced to go it alone, shunned by society that deems him dishonorable because he is a criminal and also ostracized from the community of honorable criminals.

If, on the other hand, the criminal develops a favorable reputation, he becomes an attractive choice and increases his value. Maurice, a part-time wrestler, is hired to start a fight in the track bar and be so difficult to handle that many security guards are required to escort him out of the area, and Nikki is offered "five thousand dollars for rubbin' out a horse." When Maurice hears Johnny's proposal, he asks why he is being offered $2,500 for a job that any hoodlum would gladly perform for $100. "Because I don't want any hoodlum," Johnny answers, "I want a guy like you. Someone who's absolutely dependable, who knows he's being well paid to take a risk and won't squawk if the going gets rough." So Maurice and Nikki stand to earn $2,500 and $5,000 respectively, substantially more than these jobs seem to be worth, because they are considered reliable and trustworthy professionals.

The plan calls for the group to rob the track during the seventh race, which features an exciting prohibitive favorite named Red Lightning. Nikki is to be stationed in the parking lot near the far end of the track in order to shoot the horse before it makes the final turn. Red Lightning always leads the pack, and when he goes down, the other horses are to be caught in a pileup. Meanwhile, Maurice will be seated at the bar in order to pick a fight with Mike and create a disturbance. Maurice is expected to be too much for the guards present to handle and should draw reinforcements away from their post in the nearby vault. During the commotion, Johnny Clay is to slip into a side door opened from inside by George, whose teller's cage is next to the entrance. The door leads upstairs to the employees' locker room, where Mike will have stashed a shotgun. The locker room is across the hall from the vault. Johnny will don a mask and jacket and knock at the door as though he is a returning security guard. He will herd the vault employees into the locker room, collect the money into a large duffel bag, add his disguise and the gun, and toss the sack out of the second story window to where Randy will be waiting with his patrol car. Then Johnny will leave wearing his original clothes while Randy stores the duffel bag in the trunk of his car. Randy will deliver the bundle to a cheap motel room rented by Johnny. Johnny will pick up the money and drive to the rendezvous where the crew will distribute the loot and disperse.

In *Goodfellas* (1992), veteran criminal Jimmy Conway teaches a young Henry Hill "the two most important things in life" for the aspiring criminal, which are, "Never rat on your friends and always keep your mouth shut." The aftermath of the heist in *The Killing* is upset by George Peatty's failure to obey the second commandment. George allows his wife, Sherry, to elicit information about the robbery, which she shares with her lover, Val. Val and his partner interrupt the rendezvous, but they arrive before Johnny and the money. A shootout ensues, and all present are killed, though George survives long enough to return home and shoot Sherry. Johnny and his girlfriend nearly escape to Mexico, but at the airport, his cheap pawnshop suitcase, purchased at the last minute to accommodate the entire robbery take, bursts open on the runway, scattering the money into the wind.

An unsympathetic interpretation of the conclusion of *The Killing* suggests that crime does not pay and that there is no honor among thieves. But in fact, the members of the gang performed their duties in a professional manner, and the robbery itself was successful. A sympathetic interpretation, the kind likely to be accepted by hard-boiled fiction and film noir enthusiasts, is that criminal conduct does not define dishonor; there are honorable and dishonorable criminals. The objective for organizers of criminal gangs is to distinguish between the honorable and dishonorable and to accurately identify potential teammates. Unfortunately, the obstacles to knowledge, examined in the existential epistemology chapter, render this task exceedingly difficult.

The heist film noir is particularly remarkable for its ability to obtain sympathy for the criminals and their robbery attempts. In the absence of a transcendent moral framework, crime is "simply a left-handed form of human endeavor," as Emmerich describes it. But even if conventional ethics are rendered irrelevant or obsolete, honorable criminals do not conclude that all is permitted because they are men of honor "by instinct" and because Socrates is correct about the potential dangers of dishonor among thieves, even if he is mistaken about the necessity of such dishonor. Whether or not the enterprise is criminal, there are personal characteristics and behaviors that affect the probability of success and make one a preferred associate, partner, or friend. The heist noir, in particular, presents an extreme situation that emphasizes the importance of integrity, loyalty, and commitment among thieves. The existential premise is that character is revealed under pressure. A man's honor is not determined by his occupation but by how he responds to difficult circumstances and to the temptation to betray his comrades and his own code of honor. Conventional ethical standards provide guidelines for evaluating conduct that all rational persons are required to accept, but the existential ethics of noir will not permit such an evasion of personal responsibility. In the end, only the individual reader or viewer can determine whether there is honor among thieves. The existential ethics of noir submits that the question pertains not to thieves qua thieves, but to the acts of the human characters whose individual lives are more complicated than can be captured by the ethical categories and imperatives offered by moralists.

ENDNOTES

1. "Profitable" is used in Allan Bloom's translation of *The Republic of Plato*, 1.344e.
2. Bloom translates as "interest of the stronger" (338c), though other translations offer the phrase as "advantage of the stronger."
3. King Richard is being held for ransom by a foreign government.

CHAPTER 4

THE EXISTENTIAL POLITICS OF NOIR

"They keep underestimating you."

—Butch in *Pulp Fiction* (1994)

In *Dialectic of Enlightenment*, Max Horkheimer and Theodor Adorno argue that Hollywood's mass production of cinema cannot create art. Horkheimer and Adorno's position appears in their critique of what they call the "culture industry." According to the authors, Hollywood movies can only serve the ideology of the ruling class, which marginalizes, excludes, or co-opts all that would challenge it. Directors, screenwriters, and other potential artists are converted under capitalism into wage laborers. The product of their labor is not art, but commodity. Hollywood cinema is one means through which the culture industry manipulates and indoctrinates citizens in the interest of capitalism, effectively eliminating resistance. The viewing public actually participates in its own oppression by eagerly consuming these carefully crafted products that feed their false consciousness. Every facet of movie production is calculated to ensure conformity to the studio system and further ensures conformity to the capitalist system from the citizenry.

Dialectic of Enlightenment was published in 1944 and written while Horkheimer and Adorno lived in exile in Los Angeles. The chapter on the culture industry reflects their impressions of Hollywood filmmaking made during their stay. Ironically, 1944 also marks the year of the release of *Double Indemnity*, which was crafted in Hollywood and set in Los Angeles. *Double Indemnity* represents the substantial beginning of the film noir cycle. Since the early 1970s, much scholarly writing has been devoted to these films, with considerable attention given to their artistic visual qualities and to the fact that many of those involved in their production were eventually targeted and blacklisted by the House Un-American Activities Committee (HUAC).

As we shall see, Horkheimer and Adorno could not have been more mistaken. Repression tends to generate rather than destroy rebellion, though opposition may be subtle, oblique, or covert. The achievement of film noir is remarkable because the films were rarely overtly political but offered an aesthetic existential critique of American society from the perspective of working-class males. Film noir offers what has been called a gutter's eye view of America, of how the American Dream produces working-class nightmares. Astonishingly, noir filmmakers accomplished this feat while working within the very systems (sociopolitical and industrial) that they criticized. The creative forces of film noir were successful due to their ability to artistically circumvent the restrictive forces around them. Hard-boiled fiction writers and film noir directors used the working-class sensibilities of the urban crime drama to present these critiques, and it is ironic that Horkheimer and Adorno, alleged Marxist defenders of the proletariat, were too busy creating their theory to notice the development that occurred under their very noses. Horkheimer and Adorno's judgment seems affected by a disdain for popular culture material, and their conclusions are marked by a perceptible contempt for the capacities of ordinary people.[1]

In their chapter on the culture industry, Horkheimer and Adorno assert, "Film, radio and magazines make up a system which is uniform as a whole in every part" (120). Movie production resembles factory production, where mass quantities are produced on the assembly line. Standardization ensures generic products, eliminating any possibility of uniqueness. Films are so indistinguishable from each other that at the beginning of a movie, "it is quite clear how it will end, and who will be rewarded, punished, or forgotten" (120). Why? According to the authors, film scenes are selected from bins of identical spare parts that are assembled together in a manner similar to automobile manufacturing, such that

> [t]he details are interchangeable. The short interval sequence which was effective in a hit song, the hero's momentary fall from grace (which he accepts as good sport), the rough treatment which the beloved gets from the male star, the latter's rugged defiance of the spoilt heiress, are, like all the other details, ready-made clichés to be slotted in anywhere; they never do anything more than fulfill the purpose allotted them in the overall plan. (125)

Horkheimer and Adorno contend that consumers of movies and automobiles, have, in effect, been programmed to accept and purchase these illusions. Whatever minor differences exist have more to do with the customers themselves than with substantial differences in products, as readers are told in the following passage:

> Marked differentiations such as those of A and B films, or of stories in magazines in different price ranges, depend not so much on subject matter as on classifying, organizing and labeling consumers. Something is provided for all so that none may escape; the distinctions are emphasized and extended. The public is catered for with hierarchical range of mass-produced products of varying quality, thus advancing the rule of complete quantification. Everybody must behave (as if spontaneously) in accordance with his previously determined and indexed level, and choose the category of mass product turned out for his type. (123)

The movie industry, like other industries, conducts demographics research to determine what types of plots, actors, jokes, and so forth, will appeal to viewers given their social, economic, and education levels. Those serving in creative capacities then develop and reuse formulas guaranteed to produce the predicted response. The authors are quite certain that these actions on the part of culture industry producers are completely successful, without exception (i.e., the possibility of exception is not admitted in the chapter).

The basic goal of the movie industry, then, is to crank out mass-produced rubbish to consumers who have been conditioned to accept and want rubbish. Creative professionals are required to develop ideas that appear new to consumers but are clearly within conventional boxes. Even highly regarded directors who seem to challenge conventions are actually performing the service of the industry, despite the appearance of innovation. Horkheimer and Adorno tell us that when "Orson Welles offends against the tricks of the trade, he is forgiven[2] because his departures from the norm are regarded as calculated mutations which serve all the more strongly to confirm the validity of the system" (129). According to their analysis of the culture industry, filmmakers within the Hollywood system are unable to produce movies that are artistic and challenge the status quo, and it is not possible that audiences could have the sophistication necessary to want or appreciate such movies.

Horkheimer and Adorno, to their credit, do not present an obscure definition of art, which would, using that definition, eliminate the possibility that Hollywood could produce artistic movies. Instead, they provide descriptions of the products of that system as exhibits for their position. Unfortunately (for them), the film noir phenomenon undermines their argument. Horkheimer and Adorno describe sameness and predictability, but film noir received attention, not always favorable, because the films were so distinctively different from what had come before.

It is true that studios tried to capitalize on success by repeating elements of hit moves. Warner Brothers reunited Humphrey Bogart and Lauren Bacall with director Howard Hawks to make *The Big Sleep*, hoping to recapture the romantic chemistry the actors displayed in *To*

Have and Have Not. The studio succeeded in that case, but the public has demonstrated itself to be as fickle as it can be loyal, and it is unforeseeable when they will grow weary of performers in redundant roles and tales. Moreover, if studio executives were truly able to accurately predict audience preferences and produce formula films as easily as Horkheimer and Adorno claim, every Hollywood movie would be a hit.

Horkheimer and Adorno are correct that entertainment is often targeted to certain audiences, or more accurately, producers believe that certain films will be popular with certain segments of the population. Pulp fiction was originally developed to sell to the relatively untapped market of working-class white male readers. Hard-boiled fiction grew out of the modest ambition to create realistic crime and mystery stories for these readers.[3] In order to make their features credible, writers situated tough characters in "the world you live in" of crime and corruption. The protagonists' relation to the surrounding world is antagonistic and violent, and working-class readers identified with these settings and antiheroes. The result is not passive acceptance of "the system," as Horkheimer and Adorno claim, but sympathy and comradeship with dissatisfied and rebellious characters at odds with society. The supportive response of working-class readers of hard-boiled fiction, and more diverse audiences of film noir, caused censors to worry and eventually intervene.

Contrary to the view expressed by Horkheimer and Adorno, the history of crime cinema is actually a chronicle of filmmakers' attempts to circumvent restrictions imposed by studio, government, or self-appointed watchdogs. Warner Brothers was obliged to introduce two of its most famous early gangster films, *Little Caesar* (1930) and *The Public Enemy* (1931), with warnings to the public that criminals were breeding like rats in slum communities. Censors were fearful that audiences might relate to these characters, and their fears were realized when Edward G. Robinson and James Cagney became stars portraying gangsters. Cagney's criminal characters were considered especially amiable and charismatic. The 1930 Production Code was an early attempt at censorship. Principle 3 of the Production Code states, "Law, natural or human, shall not be ridiculed, nor shall sympathy be created for its violation."

Many screenwriters and directors viewed the code's regulations not as prohibitions, but as obstacles to be overcome. As Christian Metz explains in *The Imaginary Signifier*, "The peculiarity of censorship, and one of its most noticeable characteristics, in the absence of which we would never be able to grasp its existence, is that things are always managing to get past it." Contraband slips by, "like the sluices you sometimes see at the mouths of rivers, where the water gets through one way or another" (254).

Warner Brothers Studios, the most prolific maker of gangster movies during the 1930s, was most affected by the regulations. Their filmmakers outwitted censors by mocking the code's principle that violent criminal behavior should not be glorified, and they killed off the gangster in the final scene, as was the case in *Little Caesar* and *The Public Enemy*. When censors were not completely satisfied, the Warner Brothers think-tank developed a new strategy. By shifting the popular Cagney role from gangster to federal agent in *G-Men* (1935), the film actually received the seal of approval of the Federal Bureau of Investigation, and Cagney was allowed to wield his fists and machine gun with as much enthusiasm as he had in *The Public Enemy*. Robinson received a similar makeover playing a police detective in *Bullets or Ballots* (1936), and as the word order reveals, the bullets received priority.

Gratuitous violence and sympathetic portrayals of criminals were not the censors' only concerns. William Hays, principle architect of the Production Code, declared that propaganda had no place in entertainment for which the public pays. Studio heads during the 1930s were not particularly interested in fighting code restrictions for political purposes. They were annoyed by rules that hampered their ability to make production decisions based on sound business judgment. Gangster movies were profitable, and for some reason, criminal characters played by certain actors were popular with audiences. Filmmakers were able to circumvent code restrictions during the late 1930s using socially responsible crime movies that supported the claim that poor communities were breeding criminals. These films do not openly criticize social and economic conditions, but the settings and circumstances are commentaries on these factors.

Dead End (1937) introduced a group of young tough guys known as the Dead End Kids. Gangster "Baby Face" Martin, played by Humphrey Bogart, is actually a supporting character. Much of the drama involves a youth gang and occurs at the edge of the neighborhood, which they claim as their turf. A crudely erected barrier creates an artificial dead-end street overlooking the rich section, which can be seen but not reached. The social and economic gulf between the haves and have-nots is dramatized through the Dead End Kid's conflict with a supercilious rich boy who lives just on the other side of the boundary.

In *Angels with Dirty Faces* (1938), young Rocky Sullivan and his pal Jerry Connelly prepare to break into a parked freight car. Jerry hesitates and says, "I don't know, Rocky. This ain't like stealing coal to keep warm. But Rocky replies, "Listen. What we don't steal we ain't got, right?" Even the moralistic Jerry cannot disagree. The boys are chased by police down an alley to a fence. The lightning-fast Jerry is over first, but Rocky is apprehended. Rocky is sent to reform school, and from there, the boys' lives diverge. Jerry goes on to college on a football scholarship[4] and becomes a priest. Rocky graduates from a series of prison terms and returns to the neighborhood as a notorious criminal. Rocky's and Jerry's respective situations present an implied critique of an ineffective criminal justice system. The boy who got away becomes a responsible citizen; the boy who was *rehabilitated* by the system becomes a career criminal.

Eddie Bartlett ponders his future as he ducks bullets as a doughboy in World War I in *The Roaring Twenties* (1939). "I don't want any more trouble. I've had some," he shares. Eddie's idea of heaven is "a grease bucket, a wrench, and a cracked cylinder." But Eddie returns home to learn that the promise his nation made to veterans will not be honored, and he cannot reclaim his old job as an auto mechanic. He is unable to find work but is finally able to earn a little money driving his friend's taxi during the wee hours. Eddie is arrested when he innocently delivers a package containing alcohol to a restaurant that fronts for a speakeasy. He receives little sympathy from the court, but his refusal to name names earns respect, *and a job*, from the bootleggers.

Depending upon one's perspective, *Dead End, Angels with Dirty Faces*, and *The Roaring Twenties* can be viewed as complying with the code's principles about law and order. "Baby Face" Martin is rejected by his God-fearing mother and is gunned down by police. Rocky Sullivan testifies for the prosecution and dies "yellow" in the electric chair. Eddie Bartlett leaves the bootlegging business, kills an unrepentant criminal, and is fatally wounded and dies on the steps of a church. But the crime-doesn't-pay dictum is undermined by the sympathy working-class audiences may feel for protagonists like Sullivan, Bartlett, and the Dead End Kids and by the indignation they may feel toward a system that presents roadblocks to the working and out-of-work poor.

Yes, there are alternatives to crime. During the Depression years, able-bodied men could stand in soup lines and sleep in shelters while they continually plead for work, but this state of affairs breeds anger and resentment in a nation that judges men by their economic status. Men are required to seek and find employment, but business owners are not obligated to hire them. When he cannot find a job, Eddie Bartlett complains that he is "tired of being pushed around, tired of having doors slammed in my face." As young men become frustrated and desperate, they find that one sector is always recruiting: crime. Movie criminals like Rocky Sullivan and Eddie Bartlett initially feel their actions are justified by the callous attitude that it is just too bad for them if they cannot find work. If the poor and unskilled are abandoned to fend for themselves, then, as they see it, society has no moral authority to criticize their survival methods. The Dead End Kids are also featured in *Angels with Dirty Faces*, and they idolize Rocky Sullivan because he rebels against the forces that seem to conspire against them. Rocky's motto, "Don't be a sucker," which means *don't be dumb enough to play fair in a system that cheats you*, would become the hard-boiled protagonist's unspoken response to the social and economic injustices of "the world you live in" reflected in film noir.

The evolution of the criminal protagonist as critical agent continued with the transitional *High Sierra*, discussed in the chapter on the existential ethics of noir. *High Sierra* substantially changed the crime movie landscape, and movement around the censors became more sophisticated and artistic. During the 1930s, Humphrey Bogart mostly played heavies, as he did in *Dead End, Angels with Dirty Faces*, and *The Roaring Twenties*, but he became famous through his association with film noir.[5] The shift from Cagney to Bogart as Warner Brothers' top star was significant as the style of crime films changed, in part, to suit the developing persona of Bogart.

Cagney's characters were gregarious and generous men one can easily imagine as productive and cooperative members of society—if opportunities were not denied. In contrast, Bogart's noir protagonists were brooding, pessimistic loners already alienated from a world they perceived as irredeemably corrupt. Their cynicism and moral ambiguity were acceptable because they appeared to represent values higher than those practiced and preached by social and political leaders. Moviegoers suspected, like Captain Renault stated in *Casablanca* (1942), that underneath that cynical shell, Bogart's characters were sentimentalists. Bogart could say, "I stick my neck out for nobody," as he did as Rick Blaine in *Casablanca*, or reply that his political sympathies are "minding my own business," as he did as Harry Morgan in *To Have and Have Not* (1944), and viewers would understand the disillusioned idealism. Audience receptivity to these alienated characters, as Bogart's immense popularity confirms, implies a shared vision of American society as rotten to the core. These protagonists and their vision of the world, accepted by the public, would become useful models of criticism for noir filmmakers.

Rick Blaine and Harry Morgan are expatriates who, for unshared reasons, cannot return to the United States. Their native land is not criticized directly, but once they are shown to be honorable men, their exiles arouse curiosity. Why would men of integrity be estranged from their homeland? Blaine's documented actions on behalf of underdog causes bring him under the watchful eye of Nazis in *Casablanca*. "We have a complete dossier on you," Major Strasser reports. Morgan's friendship with Gerard, secret leader of the French resistance in Martinique, draws the suspicion of Vichy authorities in *To Have and Have Not*. Blaine and Morgan are presented as enemies of fascists and defenders of "American values," yet they have deliberately separated themselves from America as though they could no longer live in a land that had betrayed those ideals.

The Bogart characters in dark but romantic adventure films like *Casablanca* and *To Have and Have Not* develop into a more noir-ish protagonist in *Key Largo* (1948).[6] Blaine and Morgan eventually set aside their cynicism and indifference to help resistance leaders escape capture. Though he describes himself as "no good at being noble," Blaine sacrifices personal happiness with Ilsa for the greater good and joins the war effort. Morgan's motivation to fight the enemy is less clear, and he tells Gerard, "Maybe it's because I like you. Maybe it's because I don't like them." Both films end on hopeful notes. In *Key Largo*, Bogart's Frank McCloud declares, "All I care about is me, me and mine. I fight nobody's battles but my own." Unlike the earlier characters, McCloud freely talks about the causes of his alienation, and we learn that his permanent pessimism is based on his insight into the corruption and hypocrisy of American society.

Frank McCloud is a former World War II officer visiting the Florida Keys to pay his respects to the father and widow of one of his soldiers, George Temple, killed in the line of duty. Gangster Johnny Rocco and his men are staying at James Temple's hotel, which is otherwise closed for the season, posing as vacationing businessmen. When Rocco is identified by a young deputy sheriff named Sawyer, he holds the Temples, McCloud, and Sawyer hostage as he awaits his meeting with a Miami criminal gang.

The Temples recognize Rocco's name, and McCloud offers the following biographical sketch. "Rocco was more than a king, he was an emperor," McCloud testifies, "His rule extended over beer, slot machines, the numbers racket, and a dozen other forbidden enterprises. He was master of the fix. Whom he couldn't corrupt he terrified. Whom he couldn't terrify he murdered." Rocco was deported as an undesirable alien but intends to finance his return to power with the profits from his forthcoming business transaction. Temple assures Rocco, "You ain't coming back. We rid ourselves of your kind once and for all."

McCloud does not share Temple's confidence because he understands the nature of the relationship between Rocco and the American system. Temple warns Rocco, "When the time comes when your kind can walk the city streets in daylight with nothing to fear from the people... ." "The time has come, Mr. Temple. It's here," McCloud interrupts, sarcastically adding, "You're hopelessly old-fashioned. Your ideas date back years. You're still living in the time when America thought it could get along without the Johnny Roccos. [Turns to Rocco.] Welcome back, Rocco. It was all a mistake. America is sorry for what it did to you."

McCloud harbors no illusions about America's ability or willingness to rid itself of Rocco's kind. He remarks to Rocco, "I had hopes once but I gave them up." McCloud says he had hoped for a world in which "there was no place for Johnny Rocco." Rocco calls McCloud's bluff, tosses him a gun, and tells him that he now has his chance. McCloud can eliminate Rocco, but only at the cost of his own life. McCloud thinks it over, then declines. "Me die to rid the world of a Johnny Rocco? No thanks," he snaps. Nora Temple accuses McCloud of cowardice, but McCloud insists that though he was afraid, fear was not the reason he did not pull the trigger. "What do I care about Johnny Rocco? Whether he lives or dies? Let him come back to America if he wants to. Let him be president," McCloud bellows.

McCloud understands that criminals like Rocco are only symptoms of the American disease. Organized crime could not exist without the cooperation, bought and paid for, of vast numbers of authorities in high places. Outlaws are used as scapegoats by police, politicians, and judges in league with powerful criminals, even as these representatives of the people offer platitudes about morality and campaign for law and order. Petty crooks are arrested and prosecuted while the foremost villains are protected from indictment. These public officials are actually themselves lawbreakers masquerading as respectable citizens, just as Rocco and his men impersonated these roles before he was recognized. Killing *one* Rocco would have little, if any, effect on the system that is apparently willing to welcome him home if he can pay the price of readmission. If Rocco were president, the nation would at least be less hypocritical.

But given the actual state of affairs, McCloud concludes, "[O]ne Rocco, more or less, isn't worth dying for."

McCloud remarks that he joined the war effort because he believed the following words, "But we are not making all this sacrifice of human effort and human lives to return to the kind of world we had after the last world war." The war was intended to rid the world of "ancient evils and ancient ills," but many film noir veterans returned to discover that while they were fighting and their mates were dying overseas, criminals and their respectable business partners were solidifying their networks and accumulating wealth at home. The new enemy is not foreign, but domestic. Dissent in the form of organized opposition is considered un-American, so the alternatives are membership or detachment, and McCloud has chosen the latter. Since his return from the war, McCloud has moved restlessly through cities and occupations, unable to find anyplace that feels like home. McCloud's experience presents the existentialist vision of the isolated individual in a world rendered meaningless.

Given these realities, McCloud has no interest in reenlisting in any crusade for justice. He challenges Rocco twice, once to give the gangster's pitiful alcoholic mistress a drink and, finally, when Rocco forces him to pilot a small boat back to Cuba. The first incident helps Nora Temple realize that McCloud is not cowardly, but in the manner of the noir existentialist, he responds only when his personal code requires him to act. Rocco promises the suffering Gaye Dawn a drink in return for a song, then reneges after she humiliates herself. Though McCloud's rational conclusion was, "[O]ne Rocco, more or less, isn't worth dying for," he risks his life to comfort the demeaned woman. "He might have killed you, but that didn't matter, you had to help her," Nora expresses, "Your head said one way, but your whole life said another." Nora agrees that the world may be rotten but insists that the just cause is not lost as long as someone is willing to fight. "I'm not that someone," McCloud replies. He eventually fights Rocco and his men to save himself, for Rocco surely intends to kill him once they reach Cuba. McCloud does not interfere with Rocco's criminal plans because it would be futile to do so. He finds Rocco repulsive, but no more so than the society that publicly rejects and secretly embraces the gangster.

During the 1940s, *Screen Guide for Americans*, published by the Motion Picture Alliance for the Preservation of American Ideals and developed with the sanction of the House Un-American Activities Committee (HUAC), had the attention of the heads of the major studios. The booklet counseled studio executives against smearing big business, financial success, and the free enterprise system at a time when the communist threat was being articulated by Senator Joseph McCarthy. Nevertheless, under these explicit restrictive conditions, several noir films appeared which surreptitiously condemn the relentless drive for material success that serves as the engine of capitalism. *The Maltese Falcon* offered a similar critique using a gallery of rogues but did so within John Huston's hermetically sealed world of interiors. One of the greatest artistic achievements of the film noir cycle presents its criticism over a more expansive canvas.

Force of Evil (1949), based on Ira Wolfert's novel, *Tucker's People*, alleges that American capitalism in the form of big business and organized crime share a common philosophy, methodology, and language. Protagonist Joe Morse is lawyer to gangster-cum-businessman Ben Tucker. They are under pressure to maintain a legitimate front because the district attorney is investigating Tucker for racketeering. Morse and Tucker have a plan to take over the numbers racket by bankrupting the independent operators, absorbing some into the combination run by Tucker. Each July 4th, millions of gamblers superstitiously bet the number *776*. This time Tucker is fixing that number to hit. The small numbers banks will not be able to cover those winning bets and will have to accept Tucker's control or be forced out of business. Meanwhile, Morse is using his legal savvy and Tucker's political connections to have the numbers racket, also called "policy," declared a legal lottery. If Tucker's plan is successful, he will own a legal gambling empire.

According to the philosophy of big business and organized crime expressed in *Force of Evil*, the aim of life is to secure riches. Joe's voiceover explains, "I wanted to be a success, to get ahead in the world, and I believed there were three ways to do it. You could inherit a fortune, you could hard all your life for it, or you could steal it. I was born poor and impatient." Joe describes the intoxicating power of riches available for the taking. "I could feel money spread all over the city like air," he says, "I could breathe the smell of money." Finally, Joe uses a form of natural law to justify the relentless pursuit of affluence. "To go to great expense for something you want. That's natural," he explains, "To reach out and take it. That's human. That's natural." The towering Wall Street skyscrapers that surround Morse as he narrates are monuments to the power of capitalist methods of appropriation.

Joe's older brother, Leo, operates a small numbers bank in a tenement apartment in the brothers' old slum neighborhood. As a business favor to Joe, Tucker has agreed to preserve Leo's bank and assign it the number-one position in the combination, but Leo refuses the offer. Leo manages his bank "the way another man runs a restaurant or bar," and wants nothing to do with Tucker, whom he considers a gangster. "I run my business honest and respectable!" Leo shouts. But Joe reminds Leo that his business is called "policy" just like Tucker's. "Don't you take the nickels and dimes and pennies from people that bet just like every other crook big or little in this racket?" Joe asks, "They call this racket 'policy' because people bet their nickels on numbers instead of paying their weekly insurance premiums."

According to Joe, Leo's refusal of Tucker's offer is a sign of weakness. "You know why you don't want it?" Joe asks, "I'll tell you why. Because you're a small man, because if it's a small thing you're a tiger, you're a tiger. But if it's a big thing, you shake your fist and call me names." Even worse, Leo's rejection of a proposition that would make him a rich man is contrary to nature and therefore evil. Joe exclaims, "It's a perversion. Don't you see what it is? It's not natural…to get your pleasure from not taking, from cheating yourself deliberately like my brother did today…from not getting, from not taking—Don't you see what a black thing that is for a man to do?" Leo's attitude is similar to that of small-time, independent criminals discussed in the chapter on the existential ethics of noir. He does not justify his criminal activity, and confesses, "[S]ometimes a man does things he'd prefer not to do." Unable to earn an honest dollar in a dishonest world, Leo tries to maintain his integrity and compensates by running his illegal business "honest and respectable."

Joe's willingness to "reach out and take it" is perceived by him as a certain kind of strength. If you can't lick 'em, join 'em, is Joe's policy. "He [Tucker] opened his pocket and I jumped in head first," Joe confesses, "I didn't have enough strength to resist corruption, but I was strong enough to fight for a piece of it." The law-of-the-jungle philosophy encourages the use of aggression to achieve one's financial goals. The powerful aggressively grab, rather than passively wait, for success. The view that it is human, natural, and justified to reach out and take it leads to the methodology of organized crime as big business.

Force of Evil submits that capitalism promotes greed through ruthless competition and acquisition. Joe introduces Tucker's proposition to Leo as the act of a grateful man repaying a debt. "Leo," he says, "I've come to take you out of this airshaft and put you in a real office, in a real business, to pay you back for everything, because you're my older brother." But when Leo balks, Joe reveals the true nature of the offer:

> Something very serious is about to happen to your business. You're one of twenty or thirty numbers banks in the city, one of the small ones. Suppose a combine moves in, suppose it organizes and merges these banks, eliminating the little one like yours. You're listening now, aren't you? Suppose it reduces the overhead, legal fees, bail bonds, suppose it reduces the costs and guarantees the profits. A man like you could be out of business, wouldn't you? You couldn't compete, could you?

Joe explains that if Leo accepts the proposal, "in return for the organization and service, in return for taking you into the combination, the corporation gets two thirds of the profits and you get one third, but on the other hand..."

Leo interrupts because he recognizes that this proposition is actually "an offer he can't refuse."[7] Either he accepts Tucker's proposal and gives two thirds of his profits to the corporation, or he will be driven out of business. Leo describes Joe's use of leverage as "blackmail," but it is actually extortion described in the language of big business. The "combination" is the film's term for organized crime. Near the end of his speech, Joes uses the terms "combination" and "corporation" interchangeably, indicating that their methods for acquisition are identical. Joe is lobbying to have the numbers racket declared a legal lottery in which the government (another criminal entity and business partner) will receive a percentage of the profits. By joining the combination "Tucker'll make you honest, Tucker'll make you respectable," Joe insists to Leo. If Joe's lobbying is successful, the combination will be classified as a legal corporation, indicating that the difference between a criminal enterprise and an "honest and respectable" business is merely technical, transformed by the stroke of a pen by officials in league with the combination.

The similar methods of organized crime and big business are further illustrated when Freddy Bauer, Leo's head bookkeeper, attempts to quit on July 5th, one day after the merger. Leo warns him, "You've got eyes, Freddy, you can see for yourself. I'm not alone in business anymore." Freddy has indeed looked around and he is frightened by the gangster presence in Leo's offices. The combination cannot afford to lose Bauer, but Leo cannot change his mind. When Joe approaches, Leo remarks that he does not have "the stomach for this kind of business." "What do you mean *this* kind of business?" Joe snaps, "Every organization has to rely on its people when it needs them." Joe calls Bauer aside and offers to "straighten out whatever trouble there seems to be." Bauer replies that he simply wants to quit. Joe asks, "Why go out of your way to make trouble for yourself? We're reorganizing the whole business now. We need every man's loyalty." When Bauer insists, "[Y]ou can't make me stay," and asks, "How are you going to stop me?" Joe turns to another company representative. Johnson flatly tells Bauer, "The combination will stop you, Bauer. Stop you dead…in your tracks."

Using the methodology and language of big business, the combination successfully executes a hostile takeover of Leo's operation. During the conference, Joe does not explicitly threaten Bauer but explains the situation in business terms and makes Bauer an offer he can't refuse. The company is reorganizing and, like any other business, needs its employees' loyalty. When Johnson intervenes, he confirms Joe's position but refers to the business as the combination, confirming the essentially criminal nature of the corporation. Once Bauer agrees to remain with the firm, Johnson assumes a paternal manner, which is ostensibly comforting but actually menacing. Johnson escorts Bauer into the kitchen, telling him, "If you have any more trouble, just let me know, and I'll try to straighten it out for you. That's my job."

Joe's position that the combination is like any corporation leads him to use a businesslike approach to his responses to Leo and Bauer. He is indignant when Leo refers to the combination as "this kind" of business. Bauer receives a similar reaction from Wally, a representative of Bill Ficco, Tucker's former bootlegging partner, when Wally approaches the disaffected bookkeeper to arrange a meeting between their respective bosses. When Bauer says, "I don't want to have anything to do with gangsters," and walks away, Wally calls out, "What do you mean gangsters? It's business." Since the methods and language of organized crime are analogous to those of big business, Joe and Wally are insulted that their *legitimate* activities are disparagingly characterized.

Wally introduces himself to Bauer as the "competition," demonstrating that the capitalist competitive battle for money and power never ends. Joe persuaded Tucker to distance himself from Ficco as they combat the district attorney and lobby to legalize the numbers racket. Now "poor and impatient," Ficco wants a place in the combination and is ready to "reach out and take it." Ficco provides the following justification for his business plan. "I was on the outside, Ben, with a gun, and broke," he says, "You was on the inside with the money and the organization. I wanted in." At the *meeting* Bauer finally agrees to arrange, Leo is kidnapped by Ficco's men led by Wally, and Bauer is killed. "TUCKER-FICCO WAR: 1 DEAD, 1 KIDNAPPED. LEO MORSE SNATCHED; BOOKKEEPER SLAIN" appears in the headlines, and to avoid more bad publicity for the fledgling corporation, Tucker is forced to accept Ficco into the combination.

Any remaining cosmetic distinctions between the corporation and the combination dissolve when Joe learns of his brother's abduction, rushes to Tucker's home, and finds Ficco there. Ficco is concerned that he cannot "do business" with Joe because of his actions regarding Leo, but Tucker is confident the dispute can be settled. They are business-men, after all. Tucker instructs Ficco to release Leo in the morning, but unfortunately Ficco cannot comply: Leo is dead. As the men violently argue, each is shown moving a hidden gun into easy reach. Suddenly, Joe sweeps the lamp from the desk, plunging the room into darkness, and the executive meeting is underway. As we have seen throughout the film, business disputes, like criminal conflicts, are settled by force.

Joe's argument prevails, and he leaves Tucker's office, stepping over two dead bodies, in search of Leo's discarded corpse. The camera follows Joe as he descends to the rocks near the river by the lighthouse under the bridge. Joe's voiceover expresses his feelings as he approaches Leo's body tossed among the weeds and rubbish. "And naturally I was feeling very bad there as I went down there," he says, "I just kept going down and down there. It was like going down to the bottom of the world…to find my brother. I found by brother's body at the bottom there, where they had thrown it away on the rocks by the river, like an old dirty rag nobody wants. He was dead…and I had killed him."

In some respects, *Force of Evil* follows the pattern established by the classic gangster movies of the 1930s. Many of the most famous films depict the tough street hoodlum's rise to the top of a crime organization and conclude with his extermination and the message that crime does not pay. *Force of Evil* retains the rise and fall formula of the earlier films but places the protagonist's existential self-destruction within a dog-eat-dog system that breeds avarice and corruption and turns brother against brother. Joe's capitulation to the crime-as-business ethos leads to an isolated and lonely existence, and his efforts to help Leo contribute to his brother's kidnapping and murder. Joe finally concludes, "if a man's life can be lived so long and come out this way," then something is horribly wrong with the world. *Force of Evil* reveals organized crime as a hideous reflection of American capitalism. The exploitation and alienation produced by capitalism are thrown into relief through the blatant actions of organized crime. If capitalism is naked exploitation, according to Karl Marx, then organized crime is naked capitalism.

Force of Evil accomplishes exactly that which Horkheimer and Adorno assert could not be achieved in Hollywood. Abraham Polonsky wrote and directed a film that provides an aesthetically brilliant condemnation of capitalism and its supporting values. Perhaps *Force of Evil*, released five years after the publication of *Dialectic of Enlightenment*, would have escaped the notice of Horkheimer and Adorno, but HUAC certainly paid attention. Abraham Polonsky was blacklisted as a communist and would not receive screen credit for many years. John Garfield, who played Joe Morse and established the independent Enterprise Studios, which produced *Force of Evil*, was first accused of sympathizing with communists, then invited by HUAC to clear his name by testifying against his professional associates. Garfield refused to give up his colleagues, but his career as a Hollywood star was over. A few years later, he died of a heart attack at age 39.

Joe Morse expresses that he did not have the strength to fight corruption but had only enough strength to fight for a piece of it for himself. His confidence is undermined when he realizes that his law partner, Hobe Wheelock, is secretly cooperating with the district attorney, but it is only when Leo is abducted and murdered that Joe finally rebels against organized crime as big business. Morse's criminal acts were his attempt to join forces with evil in a society that encourages ambitious men to "reach out and take it" by any means necessary. In some noir films, criminal acts are perpetuated not as the means to join forces with corruption, but as acts of rebellion against social and economic evils.

The opening paragraph of David Goodis' novel, *Dark Passage* (1947), captures the sense of unfairness and despair prevalent in the world of hard-boiled fiction and film noir. "It was a tough break. Parry was innocent. On top of that he was a decent sort of guy who never bothered people and wanted to lead a quiet life. But there was too much on the other side and on his side of it there was practically nothing. The jury decided he was guilty. The judge handed him a life sentence and he was taken to San Quentin." As we have seen, noir narratives are most frequently about protagonists who are cynical, bitter, disillusioned, or angry. Like Parry, they simply want to earn a living, lead a quiet life, and be left alone. But because they are on the lower rungs of the socio-economic ladder, they are subject to the discretion of those on the higher rungs as well as the randomness of existence.

Parry's escape from prison is a form of rebellion against a system that has unfairly taken his freedom. The fact that Parry received "justice" and was convicted despite his innocence, serves as confirmation (if more is needed) that the system is corrupt, and a "tough" break is the only break available to working-class men. Once in prison, Parry has two choices: He can accept his condition and assent to punishment, or he can rebel through escape, and in doing so, actually become a criminal. Parry is in a no-win situation. Rebellion is a fairly common response to conditions in the noir world and takes a variety of forms, from Roy Earle's last stand in *High Sierra* to Walter Neff's scheme to "crook the house" in *Double Indemnity*, but in all cases it involves protagonists who conclude that criminal acts are warranted in a world that marginalizes, rejects, or unfairly punishes them.

In *Odds Against Tomorrow* (1959) Johnny Ingram and Earl Slater are recruited by Dave Burke to rob a small-town bank in upstate New York. This film noir, the last of the original cycle, is ostensibly about how Slater's and Ingram's racial antagonism contributes to the collapse of their enterprise. As usual, the trio in this heist film is in desperate need of cash, but the narrative soon reveals that for each character, the robbery is an act of rebellion against oppressive social and economic conditions.

Slater and Ingram, though in trouble, consider themselves honor-able men, above thievery, and each man initially refuses to participate in Burke's robbery even before the details are shared. Slater's problems, which include convictions for assault and manslaughter, have been the result of his violent temper, not greed. When he hears Burke's pitch, Slater replies, "You got me wrong, Dave. I never stole nothin' in my life." Ingram, a blues singer, is a gambler in debt over his head to a loanshark named Bacco, but he considers bank robbery the territory of "junkies and joyboys." "We're people," he tells Burke. Burke hatches the robbery scheme, and Slater and Ingram eventually agree to participate out of feelings of bitterness and resentment.

Dave Burke is an elderly ex-cop who served a one-year prison term for contempt of court when he refused to cooperate with a state crime committee. He feels betrayed by superiors who escaped punishment and left him holding the bag. "They kicked my head in," Burke admits. He is reduced to living in a one-room apartment that he shares with his only companion, a German-shepherd dog. Bacco offers Burke a place in "the organization," which Burke refuses. When Burke asks whether Bacco's business is outside the law, Bacco answers "more or less. Everything is more or less." Burke's unwillingness to accept Bacco's offer implies that he is not willing to become a criminal "more or less" and considers his forthcoming bank robbery an isolated act of retaliation. Burke does not partner with thieves but selects Slater and Ingram, men who are not truly criminals, but who also have scores to settle with oppressive forces.

Slater is an aging ex-convict and army veteran unable to hold a job and forced to live on his girlfriend's income. His resentment is illustrated when he discovers a note from Lorry asking him to pick up her dress from the cleaners and informing him that she agreed that he would baby-sit for a neighbor. "Baby-sitter," Slater mutters to himself. An able-bodied man reduced to an errand boy and baby-sitter. On his way home from the cleaners, with Lorry's dress slung over his shoulder, Slater stops at a corner bar in a small act of rebellion.

Inside, a young soldier is demonstrating jiu-jitsu to a quartet of impressionable teenagers. The soldier tells his audience that this form of self-defense is "atom war stuff," the first thing taught to modern fighting men. When the soldier accidentally throws one of the boys toward him, Slater hurls an insult and an argument ensues. "You'd better go back and play with the girls," Slater jeers, "Tell 'em all about Sputnik." The soldier dares Slater to throw a punch, offering to show the "old veteran" that his new and improved training is legitimate. Slater answers, "That stuff belongs to my war. You can take it to Canaveral and launch it." The bartender attempts to restore calm, but the soldier mockingly says,

"It's just a scientific experiment. We're just a couple of scientists." Slater accepts the challenge. He jabs with a left, which the soldier blocks, then quickly follows with a right to the belly that drops the soldier to his knees. Slater's satisfaction quickly turns to remorse as the horrified teenagers gather around the fallen soldier.

The soldier behaved like a jerk, but as the bartender tells Slater, "the kid was just showing off." Unfortunately, the soldier's very presence is antagonizing to Slater. The soldier represents youth, potential, and the future, just as Slater feels disregarded and disrespected in a world that no longer has any use for him. Slater's caustic references to Sputnik and Canaveral, and his reaction to the "scientific experiment," indicate his hostility for the advancing space age that renders older, uneducated men obsolete by their own nation.

Slater's second act of rebellion occurs when Helen, the neighbor with the baby-sitting need, drops by to see Lorry. Helen had stopped by that afternoon to confirm the arrangement, only to have the door slammed in her face by the angry Slater. Now Slater is pleased to inform the flirtatious Helen that Lorry is out for the evening, and he is ready to "kiss and make up." Helen is pleased to inform Slater that her "louse of a husband" went to the show with one of the boys when they could not get a sitter. Slater invites Helen in, and she asks permission to ask a personal question. "How did it feel when you killed that man?" Helen wants to know, referring to Slater's manslaughter conviction. Slater replies that though the act frightened him, he enjoyed it. Why did Slater kill him? "He dared me, just like you're doing now," Slater tells the quivering Helen. As Helen retreats slightly, Slater catches her belt; her rope opens revealing sexy lingerie. She moves closer to Slater, and as their lips come together she whispers, "just one time."

The episode with Helen, like the one with the soldier, illustrates that Slater commits acts of rebellion when he perceives challenges to his masculinity. Though Slater loves Lorry and is constantly reassured by her, his inability to provide for them makes him feel inadequate and impotent. Because Slater is not responsible for Helen, his social and economic failures do not affect his performance with her. In fact, his confidence increases when she refers to the killing, which Slater evidently associates as a substitute display of potency. Helen's sexual attraction to Slater's violent history confirms the means he can use to recapture his virility. He can steal "just one time" and recover his lost manhood.

Slater is angry with a society that continues to punish aging men who have made mistakes by constricting their opportunities even after they have paid their debt to society. Slater confesses that he has been impatient with jobs that were "too slow." "I'm getting old," he tells Lorry, "I've got to make it now. And I've got to make it anyway I can." Slater feels he is being forced to retire before he has had a career. He bitterly declares, "They're not going to junk me like an old car." In this case, "they" signifies the invisible machine that uses poor, uneducated men as spare parts until they are considered old and useless and then tosses them onto the scrap heap. The machine treats Slater as an over-the-hill veteran and dares him to fight back, just as the soldier did unwittingly. The robbery, as an act of rebellion, permits Slater to take matters into his own hands and thereby recover his sense of honor. Even if he is captured or loses his life, as he is likely to do given the odds against tomorrow, the transgression affords some limited measure of self-respect.

Johnny Ingram's mounting gambling debt to Bacco motivates him to join Burke's robbery crew, but his rebellion is well underway when Burke summons him. Ingram is a handsome and successful playboy, wears fine clothes, and drives an expensive sports car. Nevertheless, Ingram is as bitter and resentful as Slater. Ingram is angry about being a black man in a society controlled by whites. If the best revenge is living well, Ingram's lifestyle is a rejection of rectitude and obedience. The "good" Negro worthy of assimilation into white society is a proper husband and father, disciplined employee, and God-fearing church member. Ingram is divorced, a weekend father, sings the devil's music in a nightclub, smokes and drinks, and cannot resist betting on horses.

Ingram's feelings about the *white* world, the only world, are revealed during an argument when his ex-wife, Annie, regrets that she had not been "tough enough" to reform her husband's bad habits. "For what?"

Johnny asks, "To hold hands with those ofay friends of yours?" Annie replies that she is trying to "make a world fit for [their daughter] to live in. It's a cinch you're not going to do it with a deck of cards and a racing form." But Ingram believes Annie is deluding herself. "Why don't you wake up? It's their world and we're just living in it," he tells her. Because virtually all whites have dangerous or suspect intentions toward blacks, Ingram can find no relief. Later that night, at the nightclub where he works, he sings the following:

> Believe me, pretty mama,
> It's not just me, I know.
> Believe me pretty mama,
> It's not just me, I know.
> I just can't make that jungle,
> Outside my front door.

Odds Against Tomorrow resembles the rebellion model of 1930s gangster films like *Angels with Dirty Faces* and *The Roaring Twenties*, in which social forces turn the protagonists toward thievery, but updates the conditions against which the protagonists rebel. Rocky Sullivan and Eddie Bartlett were affected as poverty-stricken or unemployed young men; Slater and Burke struggle against a society that offers no second chances for aging men; Ingram, against a nation that holds the promise of racial equality just out of reach.

Sweet Smell of Success (1957) is a rare legitimate film noir that is not about criminals "in the usual sense of the word" but nevertheless creates a criminal atmosphere that, like *Force of Evil*, illustrates the resemblance between crime and business. The movie is set in the city that never sleeps and presents a world in which working men must relentlessly hustle just to survive. Sidney Falco is a press agent, one of several insecure occupations available to working-class men who desire some degree of autonomy. His income is dependent upon fees obtained from publicity-seeking clients. Unfortunately, the press agent is also dependent upon columnists for publicity space, which produces an asymmetrical relationship. Falco is locked in a losing battle with powerful syndicated columnist J. J. Hunsecker, whose newspaper space he desperately needs. After many years of struggle, with little to show for it, Falco decides, "[T]he best of everything is good enough for me," and he embraces the theology of the fast buck." He performs despicable acts to maintain his precarious link to the egomaniacal Hunsecker but justifies his activities as rebellion against a dog-eat-dog system that forces men like him to "jump through burning hoops like a trained poodle" to curry the favor of those who control their ability to earn a living.

Falco confirms Hunsecker's power to make or break press agents when the columnist accepts a call at his restaurant table, at which his guests include a senator. The calling agent presents an item about his client and Hunsecker tells him, "You haven't been following the column. That item appeared last week." "Do you believe in the death penalty?" Falco asks the senator, "Because a man has just been sentenced to death." After another agent is abruptly brushed off by Hunsecker, the senator asks Falco to clarify the relationship between press agents and columnists. "Don't you help columnists by furnishing them with items?" he asks. "Sure," Falco replies, "A columnist can't do without us, except that our good and great J. J. forgets to mention that." In theory, the relationship is reciprocal and mutually beneficial, but in practice, the columnist holds all the trump cards. "The only reason the poor slobs pay you is to see their names in my column all over the world, and now I make it out that you're doing *me* a favor?" Hunsecker sneers. Falco stammers, "[T]hat's not what I mean," humbly admitting that he needs Hunsecker far more than Hunsecker needs him.

Hunsecker's mighty leverage is reinforced by his constant threats to crush Falco's ability to make ends meet unless he renders certain services. Evidently, Falco has performed several dirty deeds, and his current assignment is to break up the rapidly developing romance between Hunsecker's younger sister, Susan, and local jazz guitarist Steve Dallas. When Falco fails to make sufficient progress, Hunsecker refuses to take his call, saying, "You're dead, son. Get yourself buried." Hunsecker is punishing Falco's failure by refusing him space in the column until the task is accomplished. Falco is confident about a new scheme but implores Hunsecker to "stop beating me over the head. Let me make a living." Falco has to divide his time hustling for work and conducting Hunsecker's business. After hearing Falco's assurance of success, Hunsecker accepts an item in return for the press agent's recommitment but cautions him not to fail again. "Don't be a two-time loser, Sidney," Hunsecker warns, "The penalty could be severe."

Falco, keenly aware of the antagonistic relationship between working-class men and those who control the purse strings, engineers a meeting between Hunsecker and Dallas that should lead to an explosion. Falco has a "smear" planted in a rival newspaper that "an unnamed" guitarist is a marijuana-smoking communist, and sure enough, Dallas and his quintet are immediately fired from their nightclub gig. Phase two of Falco's plan is implemented when Hunsecker agrees to get Dallas' job back if the guitarist will promise that the allegations are false, and a meeting is arranged with Susan to be in attendance. Though relieved to have his job restored, the proud Dallas resents that he must accept Hunsecker's assistance, which is extended with the columnist's usual domineering style. Falco can predict Dallas' response because the men are in similar circumstances. As a professional jazz musician with his own quintet, Dallas has some autonomy, but his income is dependent upon club owners and patrons. Falco aggravates the tension between the men, tempers flare, and Dallas tells Hunsecker exactly what he thinks of him. Dallas adds that many ordinary people like him consider Hunsecker a phony and a national disgrace. Hunsecker is furious and counsels Susan to break with Dallas.

Before the meeting, Hunsecker, obsessively possessive of Susan, confesses his concern that he might lose his sister to Dallas. "What has this boy got that Susie admires?" he asks Falco. "Integrity," Falco answers. "What does this mean, integrity?" Hunsecker inquires. "A pocketful of firecrackers," Falco replies. Falco convinces Hunsecker that Dallas' integrity will not allow him to accept the favor if Dallas perceives that he is being pushed around. If Falco's plan succeeds, Hunsecker will have appeared helpful and Dallas ungrateful. Furthermore, Dallas will have insulted Hunsecker, producing an impossible situation for Susan, who is frightened and intimidated by her brother. "I never thought I'd make a killing off a guy's integrity," Falco snickers.

Falco's accurate prediction about the meeting and its consequences confirms his judgment that dealing with the devil is the only route of rebellion. Susan breaks her engagement with Dallas, telling him that she is fearful of the damage her brother might do. "At least this way I'll know you're somewhere in the world alive and working," she sobs. Dallas, a man of integrity, rebelled by refusing to compromise his principles and is the loser. Hunsecker, described as having "the scruples of a guinea pig and the morals of a gangster," is the winner. Falco, the plan's mastermind, is also a winner, at least temporarily.

When a giddy Falco meets Hunsecker at his customary restaurant table, he is surprised to learn that the columnist is anything but happy. Hunsecker is still fuming over Dallas' words and tells Falco, "I want that boy taken apart." He instructs Falco to "get Harry Kello," a policeman indebted to Hunsecker, with a deserved reputation for brutality. Falco insists that this is a line he will not cross, "not for a lifetime pass to the Polo Grounds." "Don't remove the gangplank, Sidney. You may want to get back on board," Hunsecker cautions. Hunsecker announces his plans to take Susan on vacation, and asks, "Who do you think would write the column while Susie and I are away for three months?" Falco, with a mixture of eagerness and reluctance, makes the arrangements.

During their argument over Kello, Falco tells Hunsecker that his willingness to follow orders stops short of putting himself at risk to go to jail. "You're in jail, Sidney," Hunsecker retorts, "a prisoner of your own greed and ambition." Falco acknowledges his own weaknesses but has a different interpretation of his choices and actions. He explains his motives to his secretary, Sally, who does not understand why Falco accepts such treatment from the columnist. "Hunsecker is the golden ladder to the places I want to get." Falco wants to go "where no one snaps his fingers and says 'Hey, shrimp, rack the balls, or hey, mouse, go out and buy me a pack of buds.'"

At times, Falco is disgusted with his actions but feels there are only two categories of people in the American capitalist system—the powerful and the powerless—and the latter must do the bidding of the former or starve. Falco's ambivalence about Hunsecker reflects his awareness that the columnist can break him but also might make his fortune. The only alternative to a lackey's existence, as Falco sees it, is to climb to the top of the heap by any means necessary. Falco's rebellion is motivated by his desire for riches but mostly by his aversion to the constant perils associated with working-class dependence upon the wealthy and powerful.

Had Horkheimer and Adorno argued that Hollywood produces many mediocre films, and many intended to help indoctrinate viewers, there would be little to contest. Instead, they contend that Hollywood is incapable of creating anything except conformity, and yet the film noir period produced many important films that were critical of the American success ethos and inevitable corruption. *Body and Soul* (1947), Enterprise Studio's earlier release starring Garfield, also asserts that an honest businessman cannot survive. He will either be absorbed or destroyed by an irresistible force of evil. In that film, Charlie Davis uses his boxing skills to acquire material success but is compelled to sell himself to Roberts, the sleazy gangster who controls access to a title shot. *Sunset Boulevard* (1950) was not only made in Hollywood but was set there. Screenwriter Joe Gillis exploits the delusions of former silent screen star Norma Desmond. Three months behind in his apartment and automobile payments, Gillis discovers that Hollywood is a cold town when you are broke. (What American town isn't?) Unable to beg or borrow money, Gillis considers Desmond his last resort. In *The Big Heat* (1953), Detective Sergeant Dave Bannion investigates the suicide of a policeman. When the trail leads to syndicate boss Mike Lagana, Bannion is warned by his superiors to "lay off" Lagana and is eventually suspended. Bannion is ultimately vindicated and reinstated, but his wife is a casualty in the battle against corruption. *The Big Knife* (1955) features Charlie Castle, matinee idol and movie star attached to Hoff International Studios. Castle's downward spiral accelerates when his contract comes up for renewal, and he resists signing. Castle learns that he is not merely an employee, but as Hoff's most valuable commodity, he is virtually owned by the studio. After a series of betrayals closes all exits save one,

Castle sits in a warm bath and slits his wrists. *Kiss Me Deadly* (1955) is the last private detective film of the original film noir cycle. Compared to his poor but relatively honest predecessors, Mike Hammer lives in luxury. He drives a Jaguar, and his fancy apartment is loaded with sleek European furniture and stylish high-tech gadgets. Hammer's relentless investigation of a woman's murder, conducted solely because he believes her death is "connected to something big," meaning a big payoff for him, causes the release of dangerous radioactive material. As was discussed in the chapter on the existential ethics of noir, heist films like *The Asphalt Jungle* and *The Killing* present teams of working-class criminals and amateurs whose members commit robberies to get out from under various financial pressures.

The directors of these films succeeded in slipping social or political criticism past various censors by artistically casting their reflections of American society in unlikely material, most notably the urban crime thriller. During the 1930s, 1940s, and 1950s, pulp fiction novels and their film offspring were often beneath the cultural radar screen of intellectual reviewers of *serious* art. The success of film noir, and its recent critical acceptance as a distinctively artistic movement produced within the Hollywood system, confirms the irrepressible spirit of art and its ability to find an audience. Horkheimer and Adorno claim that Hollywood movies are inferior products aimed at unsophisticated viewers. Their analysis of the culture industry suggests that they, like the early censors, overlooked the political and philosophical content of noir films and failed to appreciate the ability of audiences to interpret these messages. Fittingly, a scene in a film titled *Pulp Fiction* (1994) captures the blindness of the elite and their readiness to disparage ordinary people. After slipping past the security net of the millionaire employer he has outmaneuvered, a working-class boxer remarks to himself, "That's how you're going to beat 'em, Butch. They keep underestimating you."

ENDNOTES

1. Horkheimer and Adorno assert that "capitalist production" of, in this case, Hollywood films, so "confines" consumers, "body and soul," that they "fall helpless victims to whatever is offered them." Furthermore, the "deceived masses" actually "insist on the very ideology which enslaves them" (133–134). Throughout the chapter, the authors maintain that viewers are merely passive recipients, too obtuse or too brainwashed to perceive, appropriate, ignore, or resist the insidiously nefarious schemes of the culture industry, as the authors themselves apparently can.
2. In fact, Orson Welles was "forgiven" to the extent that *Citizen Kane* was nearly banned and destroyed. Welles was for several years virtually driven out of the industry and had three of his later films (*The Magnificent Ambersons, The Lady from Shanghai,* and *Touch of Evil*) severely edited by the studios.
3. Pulp fiction included Westerns and adventure stories and even romance pulps intended for women readers.
4. The scholarship must be inferred given Jerry's poverty and the reference to his football prowess.
5. Of course, Bogart's performance as Rick Blaine in *Casablanca* played no small part in his rise to stardom.
6. It is no coincidence that John Huston was involved in the more noir-ish films. Huston contributed the screenplay for *High Sierra*, adapted the screenplay for and directed Hammett's *The Maltese Falcon*, and received screenplay credit for and directed *Key Largo*.
7. A phrase from *The Godfather* (1971), a film that also presents the theme of organized crime as big business and big business as organized crime.

CHAPTER 5

A POOR MAN'S EXISTENTIALISM

"[H]ere's to plain speaking and clear understanding."[1]
—Caspar Gutman to Sam Spade in Hammett's
The Maltese Falcon (481)

The thesis that hard-boiled fiction and film noir constitute an American existentialism raises the issue of existentialism's development in these media during the first half of the twentieth century, rather than in academic philosophy. I say *academic* philosophy because, almost without exception, those recognized as philosophers during this historical period were academics. The thesis actually presents two questions. Why did this form of existentialism appear in hard-boiled fiction and film noir? Second, if the United States provided fertile soil for the development of existentialism, why did not some form find its way into academic philosophy during the decades of hard-boiled fiction and film noir? Answers to these questions will engage ancient and contemporary hostility toward narrative approaches to philosophy and demonstrate the philosophical value of existentialist crime narratives.

Philosophy can be viewed as a scientific undertaking concerned with asserting and challenging the truth value of propositions. But it is possible to take a wider view of philosophically significant writing to include work that offers a compelling vision of the world and human existence. The latter is often called art, but such a description of art need not mean that works of imagination are devoid of philosophical content or unable to provide philosophical insight. In other words, it certainly seems possible that art can perform the work of philosophy if philosophy is broadly defined as love and pursuit of wisdom as guidance for living. The dichotomous approach to philosophy and narrative appears early in the history of Western philosophy as Socrates[2] all but banishes the poets from his ideal state in Plato's *The Republic*. Socrates' arguments against the poets are manifestations of a battle about narrative and concrete versus systematic and abstract presentations of philosophical ideas and are indicative of the conflicting visions of the world and human nature presented in Greek drama and Greek philosophy.

As we shall see, certain themes offered in Greek drama and rejected by Plato are those that would concern writers who would be called existentialists in later centuries. In post-World War II Europe, where distinctions between philosophy and literature were not as sharp as in the Anglo-American academic world, existentialism was both a philosophical and literary movement. In fact, Jean-Paul Sartre, Albert Camus, and Simone de Beauvoir contributed novels, plays, and essays in addition to more academic work. The following discussion of Plato's rejection of art illustrates why existentialism fits uncomfortably within traditional philosophy as it developed and explains why imaginative works are often more conducive to existential themes.

CONCRETE VERSUS ABSTRACT

In *The Republic*, Socrates and his interlocutors are about the business of defining justice. Socrates will not accept Cephalus' claim that justice is merely giving back what one owes another, nor will he agree with Polemarchus that justice is doing good to the friend and harm to the enemy.

At first it appears that Socrates rejects these claims simply because these specific examples are misleading or incomplete, but it soon becomes clear that Socrates will not accept any instances of just acts by persons as helpful towards a definition of justice. Socrates wants to know what all just acts have in common because these are referred to as just. His request does not seem unreasonable until it is understood to be a demand for the "form" of justice abstracted from human activity. Socrates calls for a definition but one which is stripped of the human context that gives meaning. According to his view, human beings and their acts are not profitable sources of wisdom concerning justice.

This distancing from human affairs is exhibited in the *Euthyphro*, as Socrates challenges the younger man's claims about piety. Euthyphro is on the scene to bring a charge against his father, who, Euthyphro feels, is negligently responsible for the death of a servant. Socrates asks how Euthyphro could charge his own father, and Euthyphro makes the mistake of professing that his act is pious. Euthyphro's overconfident assertion gives Socrates the opportunity to interrogate him for a definition of piety, and Euthyphro is not up to the task, though eventually neither is Socrates.

Lost in their exchange are considerations about Euthyphro's father and the dead servant. Euthyphro declares that if his father is responsible, he ought to be charged; the family relation is irrelevant. Socrates does not respond to this claim, which seems to have some merit, but proceeds to the task of obtaining a definition of piety. Is Euthyphro's father responsible for the death of the servant? Should he be required to stand trial and defend himself? Should Euthyphro be commended for bringing the charge even though the claim is against his own father? Is Euthyphro's duty to his father greater than his duty to the state? These questions are not addressed. Defining the abstract concept, the form, takes priority over these issues. Socrates refutes Euthyphro's weak attempts to define piety, but the discussion never returns to whether Euthyphro's specific act is pious because, according to Socrates, piety must be analyzed without reference to specific human acts, and only then can the conduct be evaluated. Though the concern about piety was originally generated

from matters of life and death pertaining to existing persons, ultimately
Euthyphro, his father, and the servant are rendered irrelevant.

Socrates' approach to justice and piety is traceable to Plato's two-world
ontology and corresponding epistemology. Above the center-horizontal
line rests the intelligible world of concepts and forms; below the line, the
sensible world of physical objects and images. According to Plato, the
sensible world cannot be the object of knowledge because it is imperfect,
temporal, and unstable. Contemplative knowledge, proper knowledge,
pertains to that which is perfect, eternal, stable, and so forth and is limited to the intelligible world. As Socrates expresses in the *Parmenides*,
the forms are restricted to higher ideas such as the just, the beautiful,
and the good; it would be "outlandish" to think that there are forms for
hair, mud, and dirt, lowly elements of the physical world (130d). Plato
regards wisdom as knowledge, and knowledge for him involves objective certainty. Therefore, the physical world and its inhabitants cannot
provide knowledge of justice, beauty, and goodness. These human activities must be examined as concepts, or better still, as forms, free of the
contamination of the sensible world.

The conflict between the abstract and concrete is further illustrated
by Socrates' and the poets' conflicting presentations of the gods. In
The Republic, Socrates objects to Homer's tales in which the gods are
described as engaging in and causing unjust acts, lying, quarreling, and
fighting among themselves, scheming and meddling in human affairs,
altering their appearances for the purpose of deception, and other behavior unbecoming the gods. By applying the concept of perfection, Socrates
deduces the *true* characteristics of the god, proving to his own satisfaction that Homer's depictions are false. Because the god is good, and that
which is good cannot cause harm, the god cannot be the cause of harm,
but can only be the cause of good. Because the god is already in every
way in the best condition, it cannot be affected by external forces, has no
motivation to change itself, and has no need for deception.

Socrates' god is eternal and stable and therefore can be known through
a process of dialectical reasoning. Inspection reveals that Socrates'
god is the deification of his ideal rational man: the impossibly perfect

philosopher-king. Nevertheless, Socrates' god is described as a collection of abstract qualities stripped of humanity, just as his philosopher-king is devoid of human imperfection and therefore cannot be found in the sensible world. Socrates' intent is to offer a nonhuman god, but in dehumanizing the deity, he also removes the features to which existing people might relate. Ironically, his god is *known* but is not available for human engagement.

The poet's gods are also constructed in a manner that reflects their inspiration and are representations of characteristics found in concrete human beings. In other words, these gods behave as we observe people to behave; their qualities do not have to be deduced but are experienced through observation and direct experience. Just as Socrates enlarges the canvas from the individual to the state to facilitate the examination of justice in *The Republic*, the poets magnify human characteristics to magnificent godlike proportions to assist understanding. The poets' anthropomorphic gods are intelligible but remain somewhat unpredictable. For example, one can observe an angry god, but one cannot be certain what a god in the throes of anger will do. These human characteristics, attributed to the gods, are placed in familiar containers and are given the power to act and speak for themselves so that we might study what motivates and affects them. If we better understand these gods, we may acquire wisdom about these qualities that we find in ourselves. Unfortunately, the poets' gods share the complicated and unsettled qualities of their imperfect human models, and their actions confound and frustrate attempts to attain certainty about them.

The poets' gods are not perfect rational specimens, but dramatizations of discernable human characteristics that present the sometimes bewildering complexity of what is commonly called *human nature*. For Plato, a person is just *or* corrupt, courageous *or* cowardly, wise *or* foolish.[3] As abstract concepts, these qualities are treated as discrete contraries, but as human traits, they are much more tangled and confused. The poets' presentations suggest that a person can be just *yet* corrupt, courageous *yet* cowardly, wise *yet* foolish, rational *yet* irrational. These characteristics are presented as intricately related constituents of the human being, not as binaries to be divided and the offending half denied, removed, or conquered. Socrates' abstract god can only be understood as good; by contrast, in the tales of the poets, the gods are capable of acts that can be judged as good or bad or ambiguous.

Socrates' critique of Achilles illustrates differences between the positions of Plato and the poets. In the *Republic*, Socrates objects to Homer's passage in the *Odyssey* in which Achilles declares that he would rather be a slave to the living than a ruler over the dead. According to Socrates, soldiers are unlikely to courageously fight to the death in battle if they accept Achilles as a model and would prefer to be captured than killed. In this example, the fear is specific, but fear, in general, is to be avoided among those requiring courage because fear and courage are considered incompatible contraries. Given the legendary exploits of Achilles, it is difficult for Socrates to claim that the warrior is simply cowardly. So how can a warrior who expresses fear of death be courageous, for war carries the constant risk of death?

Socrates seems unwilling to acknowledge that it is possible to be fearful of death yet courageous. This combination is contradictory when its components are treated as abstract concepts, but this ambiguous complexity is characteristic of human nature. How are we to account for courage and fear except to admit that human beings possess a tapestry of interwoven traits? Socrates' position about the oppositional relationship between courage and fear suggests that he believes that courage is the absence of fear, even as he says that courage is knowledge of what to fear. The poets', through Achilles, contend that courage is action in the presence of fear, despite fear. After all, if one is not afraid, what need is there of courage?

The dispute over Achilles also demonstrates the conflicting philosophical approaches of Socrates and his artistic adversaries. For Socrates, the process by which one knows what to fear is abstract and reflective, and Socrates uses these means to instruct his listeners. In the epilogue to the *Apology*, Socrates remarks that those who *think* of death as an evil are mistaken. Death, Socrates explains, is either an eternal peaceful sleep or a transfer to an immortal place where one keeps company with the great people of the past now deceased. Socrates teaches that fear of death is overcome by the application of reason. Once death is properly understood, fear is no longer appropriate. To conquer the horror of death, one must learn to think about it more rationally.

The poets present a different view of human characteristics, which is not abstract but concrete. They could counter that the relation between courage and fear is dialectical rather than an opposition of contraries, but that explanation would merely provide an alternative juxtaposition of abstractions. Free of their human prisons, abstractions can be manipulated to the mind's content, but there may be no resulting wisdom about the living entanglement of these human qualities. The poets, using narrative, leave human characteristics where we find them, within human characters in human situations.

If given another opportunity, perhaps Plato would withhold his final evaluation of Achilles until the concept of courage could be satisfactorily defined, as his Socrates withheld judgment of Euthyphro's decision to charge his father until piety was defined. But Plato, it seems, has a problem. If Achilles is not courageous because he acknowledges fear of death, then one must account for his demonstrated ability to perform in battle. Because Homer presents Achilles as courageous, we may find it philosophically profitable to examine his courage. To do so, we will not examine courage as a form in the intelligible world but as a quality we find in Achilles.

Achilles is a warrior, and his courage is not reflective but passionate. His approach to death is different from that offered by Socrates in the *Apology*, but Achilles' attitude is appropriate for one whose warrior way of life means that the relationship with death is frequent, intense, and physically painful. Knowledge that death is simply a peaceful sleep may satisfy the armchair general, but it is of little comfort to the battlefield soldier as enemy hordes approach with swords drawn, determined to tear his flesh asunder. Even if one accepts that fear of death is irrational, the fear is no less real, as battlefield experiences and reports confirm. The poets' accounts of courage indicate that the warrior can never actually conquer or disregard the instinctive fear of danger and possible death in these living situations, yet he proceeds into combat. The existentialist submits with the Greek poets, contrary to Plato, that courage is understood, performed, and acquired in these concrete conditions not merely through abstract contemplation.

Further wisdom is offered by the poets as their characterizations of Achilles lead us to consider the issue of courage in the context of the warrior and the state. Achilles is presented as courageous yet excessively passionate, even reckless. But we must ask ourselves if it is feasible (or preferable) to go to war with regiments of philosopher-warriors. An elderly man like Socrates might rationally persuade himself to end a long life after sustained reflection, but young soldiers are unlikely to be inspired onto the battlefield, where they might be maimed or killed, by philosophical dissertations. Passionate courage may involve recklessness but is a valuable trait for any *republic* interested in defeating its enemies in war, especially during historical periods in which enemies tasted each others' steel. Soldiers are required to risk their lives and kill without hesitation, and a degree of recklessness may be required to overcome their self-preservation instincts and whatever repulsion they may feel about killing other human beings. Furthermore, warriors are not permitted to reflect about obedience to orders, the value of human life, and so forth, and then act according to their individual conclusions. This lack of deliberation has potential negative consequences to be sure but may be an unavoidable attendant of having a functioning fighting force. The poets use the drama of war and the passion of the soldier to illustrate this problematic aspect of courage. These concerns can be avoided if courage is treated as an abstract concept, but the messy complexity of courage cannot be ignored in the concrete world of warriors like Achilles.

ORDER VERSUS DISORDER

Just as Plato divides complex human experience into conceptual contraries, he also separates the tangled world of order and disorder into two worlds, one intelligible, the other sensible. The world of experience exhibits both order and disorder, but Plato elevates the half that is conducive to a more scientific approach to philosophy, and it becomes the only acceptable realm of inquiry. Plato's intelligible world provides the stability needed for his methods, and it is not difficult to understand why, for him, the instability of the sensible world and human existence is an undesirable irritant. Nietzsche accused Plato of searching for transcendence out of hatred for human life and the world of experience. One need not accept Nietzsche's psychological profile to appreciate that Plato's divided line establishes a value-laden hierarchy that, if affirmed, has significant consequences for the direction of philosophy.

The underlying quarrel between Socrates and the poets in *The Republic* is the latter's use of the world and human activity as profitable sources of wisdom. Greek tragedy, in particular, emphasizes the very qualities that Plato held in disregard: the contingency, ambiguity, and mystery of the world and the complicated and conflicting thoughts, feelings, and behaviors of human beings. According to Plato, this confusion evaporates once the world and humanity are properly understood. According to Plato, human beings (except for their rational aspect) and the sensible world cannot be known because knowledge requires certainty, and certainty pertains to the intelligible world of unchanging forms. That is why Socrates can table Euthyphro's concrete problems concerning the charge against his father and the death of the servant. But if philosophy's primary interest is contemplation and manipulation of abstract concepts and if human concerns are secondary, pursuit of wisdom pertaining to matters of existence will find expression elsewhere.

EXISTENTIAL THEMES IN GREEK DRAMA

Why did existentialism appear in the United States in the form of fiction and film? As we shall see, drama has been the preferred conveyance of the existentialist vision in Western culture since the ancient Greeks. The existentialist vision of the world is presented in works of the Greek dramatists that Socrates would censure or eliminate from his ideal state. Plays by Aeschylus and Sophocles, in particular, present protagonists harried by malevolent forces, natural and supernatural, in a chaotic and unpredictable world. Often thrust into circumstances beyond their control, these characters find themselves isolated from others by the horrors of their situations and the solitary nature of the choices they feel compelled to make. Actions taken by these protagonists to achieve their ultimate aims are mostly ineffective, emphasizing the futility of human endeavor and the unexplainable nature of human existence. Despite the absurdity of their conditions, protagonists are sometimes able to preserve their dignity through honorable acts.

In Aeschylus' *Agamemnon*, the protagonist's determination to recover the beautiful Helen from Troy facilitates a series of events that seem to follow almost with necessity though they are unpredictable and unforeseen. Agamemnon's royal hubris contributes to circumstances that rapidly veer out of control. As a result of his impulsive and reckless action against Troy, Agamemnon is forced to sacrifice his daughter, Iphegenia. Agamemnon exacerbates matters when he returns from the expedition flaunting his new mistress, Cassandra. Clytaemestra is enraged, though she has taken her own lover, and the pair murder Agamemnon. The principle characters frequently operate from passionate yet intelligible motives generated by human emotions of love, hate, anger, pride, and jealousy, and they suffer from the consequences of their own excesses.

In Sophocles's drama, *Ajax*, the central character feels cheated of the prize of Achilles' armor, which was awarded to Odysseus, and is prepared to take his revenge. Ajax might have succeeded had he not haughtily rejected Athena's offer of assistance. The insulted goddess spitefully visits horrible delusions upon Ajax, causing him to slaughter livestock instead of his perceived human enemies. Once he recovers his faculties, the humiliated Ajax can see no way out of his disgrace and decides to take his own life. Ajax could not control the circumstances that lead to his destruction and may in life always be at the mercy of the gods, but he can choose to die with dignity. Teucer returns to entomb his brother but must overcome Menelaus and Agamemnon, who oppose the burial. Odysseus, of all people, intervenes, declaring that Ajax, though his adversary, was noble in life and deserves an honorable funeral.

Aristotle considered *Oedipus the King* (aka *Oedipus Rex*) the paradigmatic Greek tragedy because it provides the best presentations of *peripeteia* and *anagnorisis*. The *peripeteia* is a reversal, the tragic consequence of human effort producing exactly the opposite of its intention. In *anagnorisis* there comes the realization of the truth, a discovery of what before was not known. Such recognition may come before or after the final catastrophe, but in Greek tragedy it comes too late to avoid disaster. In *Oedipus the King*, Oedipus investigates the killing of King Laius in order to lift the plague from Thebes. His investigation is hampered by his inability to know what has really happened. Oedipus ultimately learns that he was both subject and victim of an absurd prophesy that he would kill his father and marry his mother. The *anagnorisis*, in this case the knowledge that despite all efforts to the contrary, prophesy was fulfilled, comes long after the acts were committed, and Oedipus is therefore powerless to stop the fated outcome.

Throughout the story Oedipus is exceedingly confident in his ability to learn the truth and identify Laius' killer, but at each stage, Oedipus does not know what he thinks he knows. Oedipus knows that he voluntarily left his father's house to prevent completion of prophesy, and in one sense this is true: He did leave the house of the man he believed was his father to avoid fulfilling the prediction. But Oedipus did not actually leave his father's house because that man was not his (real) father, and he did not leave his (real) father's house voluntarily but was taken away, and the prophesy was indeed fulfilled. Oedipus thinks he knows he did not kill his father because he was nowhere near Polybus when he died, but he does not know that he did not kill his father because he did in fact kill him. The metaphysical forces and epistemological limitations of *peripeteia* and *anagnorisis* combine to thwart Oedipus' attempts to know, and his ability to act on what he finally discovers.

Eventually, Oedipus learns the facts during *anagnorisis*. Many years ago, upon learning of the incredible prophesy, Laius and Jocasta turned out the infant Oedipus, who was eventually taken in by Polybus. Oedipus believed Polybus was his father, so when he learned of his fate, he fled to avoid the outcome. On the way to Thebes, Oedipus slaughtered a man and his party on the highway over a right-of-way dispute. Needless to say, the man was Laius. Oedipus later married Jocasta, not knowing she was his mother, and eventually assumed the throne.

Oedipus is both a responsible agent and a victim of fate. He willfully kills Laius, though he does not know the man's identity, and willfully marries Jocasta, though he is unaware of the familial relation. The actions taken by Laius, Jocasta, and Oedipus to avert prophesy, through *peripeteia*, have the opposite effect and serve to fulfill prophesy. Though Oedipus bears responsibility for the consequences of his acts, prophesy indicates that he was ultimately powerless to avoid the forewarned conclusion.

Greek drama offers the tragic hero, the protagonist who is both casualty of fate and victim of his or her own character flaws, unchecked emotions, or impetuous behavior. The combination of agency and impotence, freedom and determinism, guilt and innocence, purpose and meaninglessness found in tragedies such as *Agamemnon, Ajax,* and *Oedipus the King* expresses the complex, baffling, and terrifying nature of existence. Knowledge does not provide the solution to life's mysteries but is itself problematic. The protagonists in these narratives are powerful figures accustomed to success but are rendered helpless against circumstances, supernatural beings, or fate. Each performs acts of great magnitude only to have his efforts reduced to insignificance. Each character is spirited and resolute but helplessly sinks in the quicksand resulting from senseless slaughter.

Strangely, Agamemnon, Ajax, and Oedipus, though thoroughly defeated, achieve some level of sympathy, and perhaps dignity, due to their adherence to their personal codes of honor. Agamemnon was impulsive and merciless, but he openly challenged and engaged his enemies. His murder, in contrast, was a despicable act of deceit and cowardice. Ajax was proud and haughty in his dismissal of Athena's assistance, but her response displays the very arrogance she intended to discipline. He rejected her openly, and though a goddess, she took her revenge in hiding. Athena remains conspicuously absent after the early section of the drama, while Ajax presents himself to us and attains honor in death. Oedipus was motivated to save Thebes by the promise of glory and fame, and in a perverse irony he achieved his goal. If the gods are true to their word, the plague will be lifted. Though certain circumstances were beyond his control, Oedipus does not use prophesy to evade responsibility but instead punishes his body brutally and permanently.

The wisdom offered by these narratives is that human nature and the world of experience may forever resist our efforts to grasp them fully. Greek drama does not create a perfect republic for perfectible citizens but presents an imperfect world with imperfect inhabitants. The characters, like the human beings they represent, are recognizable, but their behavior is sometimes irrational, which makes it difficult for us to completely understand their actions unless we accept their irrationality. The surrounding world is equally difficult to predict and judge. Profit and success can capriciously turn to defeat and misery. Seekers of wisdom may ask, "How should one respond to this world in order to survive, prevail or triumph?" The conclusion offered by these narratives is that there is no philosophical guarantee against calamity in a contingent and chaotic world, so one must live and die as best one can. Because the vicissitudes of life are visited upon individuals in unique circumstances, only individuals can ultimately determine how to achieve honor and dignity for themselves. Guidance is presented through the trials and tribulations of characters we admire or despise based on their conduct, not their pontifications. During the drama we are not told whom to admire or despise but are informed by lessons learned from the accumulated wisdom of humanity, accompanied by social and cultural edification, and our individual impressions.

THE BEGINNING OF THE END

The poets' perspectives were not represented in *The Republic*. Whether this omission was deliberate or an oversight, it is probably just as well. Socrates uses his dialectical method to persuade his interlocutors, and the poets would probably not have fared well in such a contest. For Plato, philosophical wisdom emerges through a dialogue in which the stronger argument is expected to prevail and its conclusions accepted. In contrast, the poets, as artists, are given to showing rather than telling. At times, Socrates asks his associates to reflect, meaning to consider or ponder, as he poses a question. Reflection has a double meaning for the artists who use imagery as a mirror. Their images serve as earthly reflections that encourage intellectual reflection. They show us ourselves, to put us in greater contact with our possibilities and limitations. The artist does not attempt to prove the *truth* through a process of rigorous argumentation intended to defeat opposing viewpoints but exhibits fragments of life that resonate with truths of existence.

Plato concedes the contingent conditions presented by the poets but reaches far different conclusions than they. The poets suggest that we must make our way through the formidable obstacles of the sensible world. Plato takes refuge in his intelligible world. His higher realm is everything the poets' world is not. It may be that the decision about whether to agree with the poets or with Plato hangs on the question of which world is the real world: the intelligible or the sensible. The intelligible world offers the intellectual pleasures of the mind. It provides perfection, clarity, and certainty. The sensible world furnishes none of these but has at least one feature in its favor. It is, to again quote Raymond Chandler, "the world you live in." Of course, Plato would not consider this an advantage, but to choose Plato's position, one is almost obligated to accept his theory of a higher reality in another world. To choose the poets' position, we need merely accept the credibility of our own experience and that of others bound to this world.

In Plato's perfect republic, the citizenry would be divided into classes: the workers, soldiers, and guardians. The guardian class consists of those citizens with the aptitude and inclination to pursue philosophy, that is to say, those with the ability and willingness to pursue knowledge of the good residing atop the intelligible world of forms. The majority of citizens would be directed into the other classes, with the prospect of a philosophical life available only to a chosen few. In *The Republic*, we are assured by Socrates that citizens with less able souls will be content with these classifications and duties that correspond to their natures.

This view seems at odds with Socrates' admonition in the *Apology* that "the unexamined life is not worth living" (38a). Socrates' expression there implies that the philosophical undertaking is the responsibility (and pleasure) of each individual, not the privilege of a selected elite.

In contrast to the exclusive nature of philosophy as described in *The Republic*, the poets' presentations were intended for general audiences that were expected to share and appreciate the messages communicated. Central and supporting characters and their ordeals were taken from history and legend. Their deeds and misdeeds, feats and defeats, were dramatized in order to teach and reinforce lessons learned in life and from life. The displays of principle by Ajax and Oedipus suggest, but do not assert as arguments would, that acts of honor and integrity are performed for reasons that are not always clear to others, even though these protagonists are driven, at least in part, by their desire to be perceived as honorable by others. Even without knowledge of the form of the good, ancient audiences of Greek drama were somehow able to distinguish the honorable from the dishonorable. Here we have the philosophical wisdom of the poets. There is no need to ascend (or retreat) to dubious and inaccessible Platonic heights that only a few (if any) can scale. Though the world of experience does not reveal all its secrets, it has much to teach us if we will pay it due attention. Furthermore, this education is available to all who are willing and eager to learn.

Plato is the intellectual ancestor of those who consider philosophy a scientific undertaking, though his approach is rationalist rather than empiricist. The world of experience is equivalent to the shadows that his cave dwellers in *The Republic* mistake for reality. According to Plato, because art deals in images that are merely inferior copies of sensible objects, it is thrice removed from the truth of the forms. Aristotle admired Greek tragedy because artists deal with concrete universals instead of the actual cases of historians, but he agreed that the works of the poets could not be philosophical because they did not deal with *abstract* universals. Though Plato did not successfully establish his ideal republic, he largely succeeded in banishing the poets from the world of philosophy. Plato's view that art cannot be philosophical, that philosophy properly involves analysis of abstractions, and (in *The Republic*) that philosophical endeavor should be limited to those few with the necessary inclination and aptitude anticipates twentieth-century developments in the United States and helps explain why the academic philosophical community was not prepared to recognize existentialist material when it appeared in the form of hard-boiled fiction and film noir.

THE PROFESSIONALIZATION OF PHILOSOPHY

The rise of academic professionalism among philosophers in the United States occurred during the early decades of the twentieth-century. This development established the philosophy professor as the official philosopher, virtually eliminating the independent public philosopher. Philosophy is identified with specialized methods and standards established by departments within universities and is recognized by professional associations. Professional status as a philosopher is achieved through attainment of the doctorate and appointment as a college or university professor. As philosophy becomes a profession, its interests, practices, and measures change. Because reputations are established by professional peers, interest in practical affairs of living gives way to more arcane and technical pursuits that are conducive to presentations at conferences and publication in academic journals. As other professionals become the primary (or exclusive) audience of philosophers, the willingness and ability to communicate with nonprofessionals beyond the university dissipates. The insularity of professional philosophy and its self-imposed separation from the public was not accidental but the result of deliberate actions.

In *The Moral Collapse of the University*, Bruce Wilshire chronicles the events that helped establish philosophy as a profession in the United States in the early decades of the twentieth century. Wilshire relates that eleven philosophy professors, led by J. E. Creighton of Cornell, met in New York City in 1901 and founded a national organization called The American Philosophical Association (APA). The association held its first meeting the following year, and Creighton, elected president, stated its agenda. According to Wilshire, philosophers were still embarrassed by Kant's charge that philosophy's failure to make demonstrable progress equivalent to that achieved in the natural sciences amounted to scandal. To regain its preeminence, or at least keep pace, philosophy would have to show "measurable increments," and to do so, it would need to develop its "own standard method of inquiry that could involve philosophers in cooperative endeavor" (Wilshire 104). Philosophy would need to reform itself by emulating the scientific approach but would also have to establish its own territory distinct from science.

The American Philosophical Association's annual meetings would serve as the model for cooperative endeavor. All too often, misunderstandings occur because philosophers read each other's work from great distances or learn about the details secondhand. Creighton expressed that the purpose of the organization is to overcome such impediments to progress through meetings in which scholars get together and clarify terms. Wilshire explains that philosophers captured their own space and their claim to special expertise by leaving to the hard sciences knowledge of the "external" or objective world, and to the humanities the "expression" of the "inner" or subjective realm. Philosophers would concern themselves with formal logic and "grapple only with problems of how implications between statements occur" (Wilshire 111).

The methods for philosophical progress were comprehensively articulated in 1912 when a "cooperative endeavor" was published under the title, *The New Realism: Co-operative Studies in Philosophy*, with contributions from Edwin B. Holt, Walter T. Marvin, William Pepperrell Montague, Ralph Barton Perry, Walter T. Pitkin, and Edward Gleason Spaulding. Section 3 of the introduction presents their "realistic program of reform," and they remark, "[T]here has never before been so great an opportunity." Logic and mathematics were the means of reform by providing the "general principles of exact thinking." Using these methods, philosophy has "an opportunity of adopting a more rigorous procedure and assuming a more systematic form" (Holt et al. 21). There would be no additional cooperative volumes by this group, but their basic tenets helped establish the analytic approach to philosophy in the United States.

The new realists offer seven principles that would provide the needed reform of philosophy.

The *scrupulous use of words* was cited as a "moral rather than logical canon." Language must be used with great precision because words are the "instruments of philosophical procedure," and the proper care of words is "the surest proof of a sensitive scientific conscience" (Holt et al. 21). Furthermore, quarrels about words are not trivial but signify a healthy intellect. The authors quote McIan from Chesterton's *The Ball and the Cross*, who asks, "If you are not going to argue about words, what are you going to argue about?" (22).

Definition involves the usage of a convention that substitutes one word for a group of words, and a convention for the reference of words to objects. The only way to avoid excessive quarrels over words is to use words judiciously, "with careful reference to their objective purport" (Holt et al. 22). The authors maintain that too often words are used "according to the capacity of the vulgar," leading to "perennial and abundant" confusion. There may be no solution to this problem except through "the creation of a technical vocabulary" (Holt et al. 23).

Analysis is defined as "the careful, systematic, and exhaustive examination of any topic of discourse." There is nothing that escapes analysis, according to the authors. If any objects of investigation turn out to be impossible to analyze, then that is because they "exhibit no complexity of structure, no plurality of necessary factor" (Holt et al. 24). The new realists note that the "common prejudice" against analysis is partly due to a "habitual confusion between words and things." This problem can be avoided only if words are kept in "working order" (Holt et al. 25).

Regard for logical form has the ability to stimulate and enrich philosophy by contributing the "form of exact knowledge." Logic deals with the same topics as philosophy but replaces popular and confused thought with the "painstaking thoroughness and exactness of an expert" (Holt et al. 26). Readers are informed that the theory of relations, logical constants, infinity and continuity, and classes and systems "concern everything fundamental in philosophy" (Holt et al. 25). These theories cannot be ignored except by the "amateur." It is proper for philosophy to join forces with logic to examine the "most ultimate concepts" such as relation, class, system, order, indefinable, and so forth, and the new realists' projects are to "extend the method of logic and of exact science in general" (Holt et al. 26).

Division of the question is essential to the program of reform because philosophical questions cannot be addressed in mass. Examination of contemporary philosophical differences must involve reduction to "debatable propositions," and that explains the need for the division of a given question. Itemization of philosophical problems reveals the following:

1. **The problem of nonexistence:** What disposition is to be made of negated propositions, of nontemporal propositions, and of imaginary propositions?
2. **The problem of the one and the many:** How many elements belong to one system?
3. **The problem of logical form:** What are the ultimate categories?
4. **The problem of methodology:** How shall one best proceed in order to know?
5. **The problem of universality:** How can that which is known at a moment transcend that moment?
6. **The problem of values of knowledge:** What are the criteria of right believing?
7. **The problem of the relation between belief and its object:** In what respect does belief directly or indirectly modify its object? (Holt et al. 27)

If philosophical progress is to be made, these compelling questions must be examined in order and one at a time. What's more, there are additional important problems such as "consciousness, causality, matter, particularity and generality, individuality, teleology" (Holt et al. 28). These concerns are generally located within systems but not as problems to be inspected and justified on their own worth.

The new realists express the need for *explicit agreement* (or disagreement) among philosophers. Unfortunately, canonical texts are problematic because their contents are "open to interpretation" (Holt et al. 28). This condition makes it difficult to reach agreement about what a text means, let alone attain agreement about the merits of its position. Proper analysis requires that "the meaning of every term must be reviewed" (Holt et al. 28). Ideally, a text should consist of "a number of carefully formulated propositions, which could be tested and debated." They conclude, "[I]f we cannot express our meaning in exact terms, in terms that we are willing should stand as final, if like the sophists of old we must make long speeches and employ the arts of rhetoric; then let us at least cultivate literature" (Holt et al. 29).

Finally, the new realists advocate *the separation of philosophical research from the study of the history of philosophy*. The problem of causality treated historically as *Hume's conception of causality* leads the inquirer to Hume's text. But the problem of causality itself leads to study of "types of sequence of dependence exhibited in nature" (Holt et al. 30). A historical approach is condemned to failure as philosophical research because of the aforementioned openness to interpretation and lack of language clarity in "classic" texts. The authors remind us that Ferrier, a Hegelian, remarked, "[W]hatever truth there may be in Hegel, it is certain that his meaning cannot be wrung from him by any amount of mere reading" (Holt et al. 31). They acknowledge value in studying the history of philosophy but contend that had history been the primary role of philosophy, there would be no history. Philosophical progress is achieved through original efforts that are subsequently studied.

In summary, philosophy is a systematic endeavor that utilizes the form of logic and the analytic processes of mathematics and science. All claims should be presented as propositions, carefully offered to facilitate analysis. All terms should be agreed upon conventions and rendered with precision. Philosophy, properly reformed, involves analysis of abstract concepts such as consciousness, causality, matter, etcetera, and the relations of these abstract concepts such as subject and object, particularity and generality, and so forth.

The new realists' imitation of science was a reaction to the failure of the grand nineteenth-century experiments of the German idealists,

Fichte, Hegel, and Schelling. Kant expected his critical philosophy to put an end to speculative metaphysics like those offered by Leibniz and Spinoza. The failure of the earlier rationalist metaphysics was illustrated by its conflicting systems, and German idealism would produce its own conflicting systems. In the cases of Fichte and Schelling, their later positions were in conflict with their earlier ones. Schelling began as a disciple of Fichte but broke away as he developed his philosophy of nature. In his *Difference between the Philosophical Systems of Fichte and Schelling*, Hegel attempted to show that Schelling's system was an advance on Fichte's, but he later caustically attacked Schelling's also. Beginning in 1829, and then for another fifteen years after Hegel's death in 1831, Schelling set about the business of undermining the considerable influence of the man (Hegel) he felt had betrayed him. Some of Hegel's own followers divided themselves into "right" and "left" Hegelians, each group claiming the proper interpretation of their master's philosophy.

The German idealists initially developed their metaphysics using certain Kantian principles. They accepted Kant's epistemological position that the subject plays a role in the construction of reality but rejected Kant's thing-in-itself, the mind-independent aspect of the object. Free of Kant's restraints, Fichte, Schelling, and Hegel were liberated to transform Kant's epistemology into an idealist metaphysic: Mind is producer of reality. When Kant described the subject's role in the construction of experience, he referred to an individual subject. According to the idealists, the construction of experience cannot be attributed to an individual subject without encountering the problem of other minds. A consistent idealism must explain the ground of experience from the perspective of universal infinite subject. For the German idealists, reality is the self-manifestation of infinite or absolute reason, and the history of philosophy is the history of absolute reason's self-reflection.

In order to transform Kant's philosophy into a consistent idealism, reality had to be treated as an activity of productive reason, and being had to be identified with thought. Idealism establishes this identification by performing a deductive reconstruction of the dynamic process of the life of absolute thought. Because idealism retained Kant's conception of philosophy as thought's reflective awareness of its own spontaneous activity, the German idealists presented philosophical reflection as the self-awareness or self-consciousness of absolute reason through the human mind.

Unfortunately, the idealists were not completely successful in their efforts to fulfill their agenda. Fichte and Schelling veer away from the direction suggested by the initial thrust of the transformation of Kant's critical philosophy into transcendental idealism. In the early stage of his philosophy, Fichte sets out not to go beyond consciousness as he establishes his first principle. In fact, his first principle is the pure ego, as manifested in consciousness. But Fichte's own characterization of transcendental idealism requires him to probe into the ultimate reality beyond consciousness. In his later work, Fichte postulates absolute infinite being, which transcends thought.

Schelling develops his thought in the opposite direction of Fichte. He begins with an absolute that transcends human thought and conceptualization, but in his later religious philosophy, he is moved to reconstruct the essence and inner life of a personal deity. Along the way, Schelling largely abandons the task of deducing the existence and structure of empirical reality and stresses the notion of God's free self-revelation. As an idealist, Schelling still tends to treat the finite as though it were a logical outcome of the infinite, but once his priorities shift to his ideal of a personal God, his thought drifts away from the original direction of metaphysical idealism.

Hegel delivers the most sustained effort to maintain the idealist agenda. According to him, the real is rational and the rational is real. By writing of the subject as individual subject, Kant represented the human mind as finite, and on those grounds questioned its ability to grasp anything like the self-unfolding life of absolute reason. Hegel asserts that mind has its finite aspects but is also capable of rising to the level of absolute thought, and at that level, the absolute's knowledge of itself and human knowledge of the absolute are identical. Human knowledge of the absolute is the absolute's knowledge of itself, as it becomes in existence what it always was in essence: self-thinking thought. Philosophy's concern is to demonstrate how reality is the life of absolute reason in its movement towards the goal of self-knowledge.

As mentioned earlier, the transcendental ego serves as Fichte's first proposition of philosophy. This transcendental ego is described as activity directed towards an activity. Self-consciousness, knowledge, cannot emerge unless the nonself or nonego is opposed to the ego. Thus, Fichte's second basic proposition of philosophy, the nonego, stands to the first as antithesis to thesis. Fichte's dialectic of thesis, antithesis, and synthesis forms the three basic propositions of philosophy. According to Fichte, the contradictions or oppositions that seem to arise are resolved when the meanings of the statements are properly defined.

Hegel argued that Fichte's synthesis was insufficiently philosophical because Fichte has to introduce activities not properly deduced to make possible the transition from one proposition to the next. Hegel complained that Fichte's practical deduction of consciousness posited nature only as the opposite of ego, leaving an unresolved dualism, and was unconvinced by Fichte's claim that defining the *thesis* and *antithesis* terms would make their mutual compatibility evident.

According to Schelling, absolute reason is the identity of subjectivity and objectivity, the absolute act in which subject and object are one. Absolute reason achieves self-consciousness in and through human consciousness. From the perspective of empirical consciousness, subject and object are distinct. But if we try to transcend the perspective of empirical consciousness and try to grasp the absolute, we can only conceive it as the *in*difference or the lack of difference. In other words, we can only conceive the absolute as the vanishing point of all distinctions.

In his *Preface to The Phenomenology of Spirit*, Hegel rejects Schelling's account of the absolute. Hegel does not accept Schelling's position that the absolute transcends conceptual thought and that we must address the absolute identity by thinking away the attributes of the finite. For Hegel, the absolute is not an ineffable identity, but it is the total process of its self-expression or self-manifestation in and through the finite. Hegel argued that to consider the absolute as a dark, impenetrable abyss, a vanishing point of all differences inscrutable to reason, is to proclaim the absolute as the mystical night in which, as he famously put it, "all cows are black."

Schelling eventually counterattacked Hegel by stressing the difference between what he referred to as negative and positive philosophy. Negative philosophy is concerned with concepts, while positive philosophy engages existence. Though Schelling's earlier philosophy was negative, he came to the conclusion that from concepts we can only deduce other concepts. Negative philosophy's deduction of the world is not a deduction of the existing world but only a deduction of what that world must be like *if* it exists. In other words, negative philosophy, particularly Hegel's philosophy, cannot account for the existing world.

Though initially motivated to continue and improve Kant's project, the German idealists neglected his aim. In the tradition of the British empiricists, especially Locke and Hume, Kant sought to clarify the boundaries of human knowledge and bridle the ambitions of speculative philosophers who presumed the mind (and their own minds) capable of capturing the totality of reality. Fichte, Schelling, and especially Hegel, produced metaphysical systems that were incredible, and for their critics, more indicative of their ability to juggle abstractions than they were plausible accounts of reality. The failure of the grand schemes of the German idealists created a backlash from more scientifically oriented philosophers, and regenerated questions about the efficacy of philosophy, which the new realists' program of reform was intended to address.

The new realists were not the only group to influence the direction of philosophy in the United States during the early years of the twentieth century. Ten years later, in 1922 another cooperative endeavor appeared, this time from critical realists Durant Drake, Arthur Lovejoy, James Pratt, Arthur Rogers, George Santayana, Roy Sellars, and C. A. Strong. American philosophers were also affected from abroad by the analytic writings of G. E. Moore and Bertrand Russell and from the language philosophies of Ludwig Wittgenstein and A. J. Ayer.

Intrepid readers who open the pages of *Essays in Critical Realism: A Co-operative Study of the Problem of Knowledge* will find themselves plunged into an esoteric discussion already well underway. The first essay, "The Approach to Critical Realism," by Durant Drake, offers a "justification of realism" and serves as an introduction to the topic (3). We are told that critical realism will expose the errors inherent in the "two historic types" of realism (Drake 4). Drake begins by clearing the path of pure subjective and naïve realism. If subjectivists are correct, we do not directly apprehend physical objects but experience the mind's representations of these objects. Knowledge is restricted to our own mental states, and we cannot know with certainty what exists beyond them, including the physical world. If, on the other hand, sense-data are "aspects of the object prior to perception," we are left to account for different perceptions of those aspects (Drake 10). In the example offered, one perceiver perceives green leaves of a tree, while another colorblind perceiver perceives the same leaves as gray. From here, the reader is led through an advanced discussion of the many subtle distinctions between various aspects of realism.

It is important to note the intimidating language of the essays in the cooperative volume. The attitude that the book is intended for professionals only is made explicit in the second chapter, "Pragmatism Versus the Pragmatist" by Arthur Lovejoy. The beginning reader who wonders how pragmatism can be adversarial toward the pragmatist is told that "some of the theses of pragmatist writers" are more *genuinely* pragmatic than others. What, then, are these various theses? Lovejoy states, "the customary formulas are presumably known to all persons who are at all likely to read this volume" (37). Thus, no effort will be made to explain matters to those without specialized expertise. The authors imply that such persons have no business reading the volume.

Persistent readers will discover there is a problem of knowledge that concerns the subject's relation to the data of perception. As they read such philosophy books, they may become curious about what any of this has to do with wisdom, especially because there seems to be no practical problem of knowledge. For example, the philosopher who proposes that time is unreal will eventually glance at a watch, set an alarm, make a dinner reservation, and so forth. Likewise, the problem of perception seems like a contrived intellectual problem, not a practical one. Because, as Drake reminds us, our encounter with the world is mediated by the mind's representation of the world, there is reason to be skeptical about our *knowledge* of the world. How can one prove that the world outside the mind exists, for we cannot know the world except through the mind? But as Santayana himself explained, no one is an absolute skeptic, except for the purpose of argument. One who suspends all action until certitude is achieved is paralyzed. We proceed through life with what he refers to as animal faith, confident, if not intellectually certain, that our experience of the world is sufficient for us to get on with the affairs of living.

Though critical realists, British analytics, and Vienna Circle philosophers influenced the direction of thought in the United States during the early years of the twentieth century, the new realists are especially important to this discussion because they were not merely distracted by, or uninterested in, philosophy beyond the university, but they made assertions about the correct content and form of philosophy. They did not claim that analysis is one method among many, each with its own strengths and weaknesses. According to them, approaches to philosophy that are not built upon the foundations of mathematics and science are not philosophy at all but are the practices of literary artists and other amateurs.[4] It is easy to realize how such views, if dominant, could lead professionals to exclude work that did not conform to these principles.

In *The Rise of American Philosophy* (1977), Bruce Kuklick soberly describes the institutionalization of these values at Harvard throughout the early decades of the twentieth century. In the late nineteenth century, Harvard attracted prominent philosophers and began building what would become the preeminent graduate program in philosophy. The institution's subsequent domination of the academic world of philosophy resulted in two related developments: The public philosopher was replaced by the philosophy professor, and philosophy's emphasis shifted away from the practical affairs of living to the technical areas of university research consistent with scientific approaches to philosophy. By establishing philosophy as an academic profession, Harvard (and the APA) effectively entrenched the standards one would have to meet to be called a philosopher. Harvard's dominance was confirmed in 1930, when *Contemporary American Philosophy* was published. The three divisions of the American Philosophical Association chose thirty-four philosophers to represent the shape of American philosophical thought. All three editors of the book received their highest degree from Harvard. Five were members of the Harvard faculty, and the book was dedicated to a man with a long and distinguished record of service at Harvard. Needless to say, all contributors were philosophy professors.

The Golden Age describes the thirty-year period, beginning in 1880, in which Josiah Royce and William James spent time together at Harvard. Kuklick explains that though Royce and James were concerned to address themselves to an educated public about practical affairs of living, they, however unintentionally, laid the foundation for the transformation of philosophy at Harvard. Royce and James dedicated themselves to the science-religion controversy created by Darwin's theories and encouraged a scientific approach to practical problems and supported their defense of religious belief with epistemological arguments. Their scientific approach created a hierarchical standard, with the technical areas of philosophy ranked highest. Kuklick relates that Royce and James inherited their outlook from Kant and taught their students, who included future new realists Perry, Holt, and Montague, and critical realist Santayana, that "solving the problems of *The Critique of Pure Reason* was the key to philosophical advance." Students may have been drawn to Harvard to study religious questions, but shifted their attention to "Royce's epistemological and logical conundrums" (Kuklick 452).

Kuklick's data demonstrate the changing interests of students and graduates from 1907 to 1927 at Harvard. During the first years of the research period, the majority of new PhDs (62 percent) cited "religious doubt or problems" in response to the question "Why are you in philosophy?" Kuklick relates that the doctoral degree in philosophy came to be treated as preparation for a career, and students came to Harvard because it was the leading institution for graduate study, rather than because it was the premiere place to address moral and religious questions. Graduates tended to think of themselves as professional experts and labored to establish themselves within the discipline and the university system. Kuklick concludes, "[B]y the third decade of the century the phrase 'professional philosopher' embodied a verbal contradiction: newly minted doctors found that the love of wisdom was only a job" (475).

Kuklick's research, provided in his chapter titled "The Professional Mentality," also shows the increase in specialization into the technical areas of philosophy (463–480). Data collected up to 1906 indicate that only 16 percent of PhDs were in technical areas of logic, epistemology, methodology, etcetera. From 1907 to 1918, the number grew to 32 percent, and in the period 1920–1930, it moved up to 51 percent. Kuklick provides evidence that graduates who specialized in technical areas found so-called better jobs than those who studied practical interests like religious and moral philosophy. Before 1907, coveted positions were fairly evenly distributed, but between 1907 and 1918, matters changed significantly. According to Kuklick's information, 30 percent of degrees went to technical specialists, but 57 percent of the eminent positions and 37 percent of the well-placed positions went to them, meaning that 94 percent of the more desirable jobs were secured by them. Meanwhile disproportionately high numbers of graduates specializing in the soft areas were merely placed or did not obtain significant positions. As more graduate students pursued philosophy as a means to an academic career, there were professional incentives to gravitate toward the areas of the discipline that promised greater success within the university system.

The APA's establishment of philosophy as a profession, the new realists' program of reform, and Harvard's dominance in the academic world placed philosophy beyond the "capacity of the vulgar" and away from the activities of "amateurs." Kuklick relates that Harvard-trained philosophers of the 1930s moved into the professoriate without ever realizing that philosophy was once significant beyond the university. The result of the professionalization of philosophy was that "love of wisdom was no longer something that men could practice when they took walks with their friends; nor was it doomed to the endless reworking of ancient puzzles; cooperative inquiry, technical expertise, a learned jargon, and a division of labor would win the day" (Kuklick 350).

As we have seen, during the early decades of the twentieth century, the establishment of the APA, the domination of the Harvard philosophy department, and the new realists' project of reform led to the professionalization of philosophy and the redefinition of philosophy according to the practices of academics. The very title of the American Philosophical Association implies that those outside its orbit are not members of the developing American philosophical community. Philosophy professors are insiders; others are considered outsiders. The APA's agenda, to emulate the scientific approach, easily dovetailed with the new realists' program of reform, and its insistence that definition, analysis, and logic are the only proper territory of philosophical inquiry and discussion. While the APA's designation and affirmative agenda implicitly eliminates outsiders, the new realists explicitly stated that nonscientific approaches should *not* be considered philosophy, and those engaged in such practices were litterateurs or amateurs. The Harvard philosophy department helped to institutionalize these attitudes by conferring status as a philosopher to those completing the doctoral degree, by influencing and training a new generation of graduate students, and with their ability to assist or inhibit career opportunities. The professionalization of philosophy restricted philosophical inquiry to college and university campuses by reducing, if not eliminating, the ability for one to be an acknowledged philosopher independent of an academic institution.

The professionalization of philosophy also served to exclude those outside the academic world from participating in the intellectual conversation. William James is conspicuous among his peers for his efforts to communicate with the nonprofessional educated public; the excerpt offered from the critical realists' cooperative publication is more representative of the period. Though new realists remarked about the "capacity of the vulgar," Lovejoy's comments that the theories of pragmatism are known to anyone likely to read the volume, does not so much convey contempt, but lack of consideration for nonprofessionals. Persons interested in philosophy with neither the freedom from employment nor the tuition needed to attend campus philosophy courses have little means to engage in the philosophical conversation. Should such persons attempt independent study, they will discover that most philosophy books and articles written during and after the period of Kant (the first member of the canon to be a philosophy professor) presume reader knowledge of the history of philosophy and its complicated and sometimes bewildering jargon. Furthermore, readers will find numerous pages of logic, definitions, analysis of propositions, etcetera, unrelated to the practical concerns that drew them to philosophy in search of wisdom.

CRIMINALS MOVE IN

Criminals have often filled the void when authorities deny public access to desired goods and services. During the Prohibition era, criminals met the demand for alcohol that did not simply disappear because institutions of power attempted to halt the supply. University-trained professionals may believe that laypeople without a taste for analysis of abstract concepts are not thirsty for philosophy, but the desire for philosophical sources as guides for living in the world of experience may nevertheless exist. The difficulties of life give rise to practical philosophical questions, and the territory generally abandoned by academic philosophy was left to various *amateurs*. During the 1920s, the creators of hard-boiled fiction unintentionally responded to this need among working-class men with tales set in the criminal milieu that spoke their language. Caspar Gutman's toast to Sam Spade in *The Maltese Falcon*, "Here's to plain speaking and clear understanding," captures the approach taken by hard-boiled fiction writers to their audience (Hammett 481). What they offered readers was not the claimed exactness of propositions in technical jargon, but the vernacular that expressed their common experience.

The factors that led to the production of the existentialist strain of hard-boiled fiction exemplified by Dashiell Hammett were fortuitous. *Black Mask*, the pulp magazine that changed the face of detective fiction, was created by H. L. Mencken and George Jean Nathan in 1920 to underwrite their slick publication, *Smart Set*. Mencken and Nathan developed profitable pulps, *Pariesienne* and *Saucy Stories*, but neither generated enough revenue to pull them out of the red. The success of *Detective Story*, produced by rival publisher Street and Smith, convinced Mencken and Nathan to create their own detective pulp. The logo of *Smart Set* included a line drawing of Satan in a black mask, and they took that image for their title. Mencken made no effort to hide his disdain for pulp fiction, including his own, but moved into the arena out of economic necessity. The stories sold well, despite their poor quality, and confirmed reader hunger for hard-boiled mysteries. In November 1920, just eight months after the first issue appeared, Mencken and Nathan sold *Black Mask*[5] to Warner Publication for a healthy profit of $11,750.

Black Mask experienced rapid change over the next several years. Story quality improved considerably in 1922 when George Sutton became editor and in December printed the first fiction by Carroll John Daly and Dashiell Hammett. Phil Cody assumed editorship in April 1924 and recognized that Daly's and Hammett's detectives "represented a bold new step beyond the traditional detective school of crime fiction" (Nolan 23). Dashiell Hammett had worked as a detective for the Pinkertons, and Cody hired more writers with extensive work experience and encouraged them to inject realism into their stories. Nels Leroy Jorgensen had been a motorcycle patrolman in New Jersey. Tom Curry was a former police reporter for a major New York newspaper and claimed his stories came "right out of life." Raoul Whitfield was a licensed pilot and provided aviation thrillers. In 1926 Hammett quit over a salary dispute, and circulation dropped considerably. Cody subsequently resigned his post as editor, but his replacement would establish the image that *Black Mask* retains among hard-boiled fiction connoisseurs.

Joseph Thompson Shaw approached Cody, at this time president of Warner Publication, which owned *Black Mask*, to sell a story. His writing was rejected, but Shaw so impressed Cody that he was immediately hired as editor. Shaw knew nothing about editing[6] and had never even read an issue of *Black Mask*. He immersed himself in back issues and decided that Hammett's work represented the direction he wanted the magazine to take. Shaw coaxed Hammett into returning, and the writer spun two long stories that would become the novelette *Blood Money*.

With Hammett back in the fold, the June 1927 issue featured Shaw's editorial, "The Aim of Black Mask." According to Shaw's principles, detective fiction "had to be convincing, must be real in motive, character and action, must be plausible, clear and understandable" (qtd. in Nolan 25). Shaw intended to establish *Black Mask* as the only magazine of its kind in the field. He was contemptuous of the distinction between "slicks" and "pulps," and expressed his belief that detective fiction could have as much literary merit as any other kind of writing. To accomplish Shaw's objectives, detective fiction had to meet the "requirements of plausibility" and contain "truthfulness in details" (Nolan 25). As to language, Shaw announced that writing must convey "simplicity for the sake of clarity, plausibility and belief" (MacShane 46).

The Hammett-led strain of hard-boiled fiction uses Shaw's demand for objective realism to create a bleak and pitiless world of crime and corruption. In the language of "plain speaking and clear understanding," the existential metaphysics, epistemology, ethics, and politics of noir raise questions that address the individual's relation and response to that world from the perspective of its mostly working-class inhabitants. Contingency and powerlessness render characters' existence uncertain and unpredictable. The opaqueness of the world and human nature undermines the ability to know or understand others. Irredeemable corruption leaves ethics inapplicable. Collective resistance is classified as un-American activity. Given these permanent conditions that emphasize the absurdity of life, is there good reason to be hopeful for a more stable and secure world? Can dignity and integrity survive given such pervasive corruption? If there is indeed no prospect of change and no avenue of escape, how should one proceed?

If any character provides answers to these questions for hard-boiled fiction's intended audience, it is the private detective, for he endures, relatively speaking, more often than other types of protagonists. Toward the end of his essay, "The Simple Art of Murder," Raymond Chandler describes the working-class qualities of the hard-boiled private detective: "He is a relatively poor man, or he would not be a detective at all. He is a common man or he could not go among common people. He has a sense of character, or he would not know his job. He will take no man's money dishonestly, and no man's insolence without a due and dispassionate revenge" (992).

Chandler adds that the detective's approach to language conveys "disgust for sham, and a contempt for pettiness" (992). In other words, the private detective is an advocate of plain speaking and clear understanding, which contributes to his ability to go among common people. These qualities place the hard-boiled detective's attitude and delivery in sharp contrast with the inaccessible, impenetrable, or irrelevant presentations of many professional philosophers of the period.

Chandler's private detective, Philip Marlowe, is an especially effective model given his longevity in the genre. Marlowe's distinction among noir detectives is his emphasis upon professionalism, loyalty, and integrity, and his compassion for the rare few he encounters who exhibit these attributes. Marlowe is unusually urbane, as his detailed descriptions of landscapes, architecture, fashion, and practically everything else demonstrates, but he is quick to deflate pomposity. The "rude wit" Chandler describes is reserved for the supercilious. Marlowe's first-person narratives offer commentary from a *most wised-up guy*, grounded in the reality of the world you live in. By talking to us, rather than over our heads, Marlowe takes us into his confidence and offers the perspective of a man we can trust. His intelligence, experience, "truthfulness in details," and innate goodness make him a useful model for readers in search of, or receptive to, responses to practical philosophical questions provoked by a corrupt world.

Through Marlowe's adventures and his narrative critique, interested readers discover that there are short answers to each of the aforementioned questions. Is there good reason to be hopeful for a stable and secure world? *No.* Can dignity and integrity survive, or exist all at, given such pervasive corruption? *Not entirely, or not without other costs.* Without the prospect of change or any avenue of escape, how should one proceed? *It remains up to the individual to decide.* "Down these mean streets a man must go who is not himself mean, who is neither tarnished nor afraid," Chandler wrote of the hard-boiled private detective ("Art of Murder" 992). The world is not likely to change, so the challenge is to remain faithful to chosen principles and to be a "stand-up" guy. Marlowe's ethos of professionalism provides a philosophical framework of honor and integrity.

The private detective's experience provides longer answers to these questions and also presents the associated costs. There is no good reason to hope for a better world, but for one unwilling to join corrupt forces and too wised-up to believe that the police are ready, willing, and able to confront the enemy, private investigation provides the independence needed to shape and establish one's character. Dignity and integrity can be maintained with some loss of purity, but the private detective must struggle to remain free of the primary temptations: sex, money, and power. The detective occasionally meets those who seem trustworthy, but those associations are brief. Without the prospect of change or avenue of escape, each individual must choose a course, and private detectives are not uniform in their approaches.

The most existentialist private detectives, the Continental Op, Sam Spade, Philip Marlowe, Mike Hammer, and J. J. Gittes, have approaches suited to their individual standards. The Op treats his experiences as work assignments and keeps his distance. Spade resorts to many of the tactics of his adversaries but will not violate the standards of his profession. Marlowe, easily the most conventionally moral of the group, castigates the corrupt but takes some solace that he occasionally encounters people who meet his standards. Mike Hammer believes that might makes right, and right makes might. The system is incapable of fighting injustice and needs the strong arm of an avenger empowered by righteousness. J. J. Gittes reduces the scale of corruption to a more tractable size by restricting his investigations to "matrimonial work." The diversity of responses among private detectives confirms that individuals must ultimately answer these questions for themselves. These conclusions may be disappointing to those who expect philosophy to answer all questions and solve all problems and do so with a universal reply.

CHOICES

In his essay "My Mental Development," renowned analytic philosopher Bertrand Russell shares that he was out for a walk when he suddenly realized the soundness of the ontological proof of God's existence. Russell soon realized his error, but one can imagine the potential effect upon an atheist steadfastly committed to logic. If the ontological argument is valid and sound and proves God's existence, the philosopher dedicated to logic is required to renounce atheism. If that same philosopher later identifies a flaw in the ontological proof, he or she would then be obligated to change positions again. Such devotion to the application of reason is admirable, but the tale is not without its comic aspect.

Perhaps there are people whose religious belief is determined solely by proofs of God's existence, but it seems likely that the majority of people (including intelligent and educated people) are not persuaded to make momentous decisions solely on the basis of logical arguments. Some philosophers would argue that this is precisely the problem with the majority of people. However, if the hypothesis is correct, philosophers who regard philosophy as a scientific endeavor committed to proving that certain propositions are true have three options concerning philosophy's relation to those outside the university.[7]

1. They can write off the general population and ignore them.
2. They can try conversion and attempt to convince the population of the superiority of their methods.
3. They can use approaches to philosophy more likely to resonate with the majority of the population of nonprofessionals who fail to appreciate the value of quarreling over words.

The professionalization of philosophy has largely implemented the first option, as most philosophers (i.e., philosophy professors) spend their adult lives on campuses, moving from undergraduate and graduate study to faculty positions. At research universities, the teaching of undergraduates other than philosophy majors is a chore to be avoided and is often delegated to graduate students. Academic philosophers largely ignore those outside the university, and the general public reciprocates. Perhaps philosophers in the tradition of the new realists regard their discipline as similar to physics, with academic training intended for professionals. Physicists conduct research, and the blessings eventually trickle down to nonprofessionals who need not be involved except as beneficiaries. If so, the professionalization of philosophy and the virtual exclusion of the general public need not be lamented.

The branches of the liberal arts such as philosophy, literature, art, and music are concerned with human thought and culture. These areas of study were not intended as the exclusive territory of professionals but belonged to the educated public and all willing to learn. The humanities were once considered the foundation of liberal education, expressing what it means to be an educated person. Philosophy, defined as "love and pursuit of wisdom by intellectual means and moral self-discipline,"[8] is a valuable process of discovery, enrichment, and development and enhances our liberal democracy by encouraging humane, thoughtful, and active citizens. Philosophy's enduring ability to stimulate minds depends upon its willingness to engage difficult and relevant questions of concrete importance.

Option two, conversion, is available to philosophers who insist their academic definition is the only proper one but are alarmed and dismayed by the virtual insignificance of philosophy beyond the university. Advocates of the analytic approach, in its several forms, face challenges inherent in their vision of philosophy as they attempt to persuade others. It is unlikely that a protracted logical argument about the superiority of logical analysis will be effective with people resistant to persuasion by arguments of this kind. Yet if philosophers use other means of persuasion, they admit the value of other means. Scientific philosophers must also convince nonprofessionals that analysis of abstract concepts is relevant to their lives. Continental philosophers would also be obliged to explain how the writings of critical theorists, structuralists, poststructuralists, posteverythings, and their commentators are pertinent to the living concerns of those they wish to recruit, unless they, and their analytic counterparts, are prepared to demonstrate that philosophy need not be relevant to be worthy of extensive time and energy. They must then be prepared to explain why nonprofessionals should suffer through volumes of abstruse analysis and obscure language.

In *Dogmatic Wisdom*, Russell Jacoby confirms and expands Kuklick's speculation that the establishment of a technical vocabulary in the humanities is intended to garner the level of professional prestige accorded mathematics and the natural sciences. Jacoby reports that for academics "complex sentences spell profundity, and profundity spells professionalization" (*Dogmatic Wisdom* 168). He quotes Judith Frank's claim that "for those of us who have gone through graduate training, the humanities are a profession, and [that] the people who practice a particular profession are trained in its language" (167). Jacoby concludes that obscure language is deliberately employed to bar entry to nonprofessionals. "These tags mean: Stop. Do Not Enter. We are scientists," he remarks (167).

Jacoby's account is provided to explain intentionally "bad" writing by academics but also illustrates that many university professors bristle at the notion that the humanities should be accessible to the general public. Readers cannot expect complicated ideas to be expressed with "the leisurely elegance of a coffee-table magazine" (*Dogmatic Wisdom* 168). Jacoby shares that many academics embrace the theory that clear language undermines critical thought. Complex ideas require complex language. Philosophy, considered the most intellectual of the humanities, is especially susceptible to this way of thinking. If philosophers believe that accessible language is equivalent to "simplemindedness" and "represses critical thinking," then these professionals lack the willingness and means to communicate with nonprofessionals.

The views captured by Jacoby capture the common view that learning necessarily involves rigor, that is, torture. If texts are not abstruse and obscure, they are not worthy of academic study; if students are not suffering, they are not working hard enough or the material is not sufficiently demanding. This position is similar to the no-pain-no-gain attitude expressed by some fitness trainers. Narrative approaches to philosophy, on the other hand, are analogous to sports activities in which participants are so absorbed in play that their attention is diverted from the grueling monotony of training, and consequently the athletes increase the intensity and duration of their exercise.[9] What about rigorous training for these sports? To strengthen the wrists of shooters, some basketball coaches direct players into the weight room to perform tedious sets of wrist curls with dumbbells. Other coaches instead employ techniques that simulate sports activities and send players onto the court to shoot baskets from a chair or the court floor. The seated position not only increases the distance to the basket, but also eliminates aid from the legs, forcing the athlete to exercise the wrist. The clever coach initiates a contest among the players, and their competitive desire to make baskets from the chair or floor distracts them from their fatigue. These contests continue with considerable enthusiasm, even though the players rarely win any prizes except bragging rights. The effectiveness of training methods is measured by the athlete's conditioning, which is, after all, the objective of the training.

Wised-up basketball coaches realize that the objective of conditioning is not to compel weight training but to increase wrist strength, in this example. What is the objective of philosophy? Is it to compel students to read academic texts? Does philosophy primarily, or exclusively, involve the issues and arguments raised by those philosophers admitted to the canon? Is philosophy a strictly scientific endeavor concerned with abstract technical problems such as those outlined by the new realists? If the answer to these questions is "yes" or "YES!" then it may be appropriate to treat philosophy accordingly, though we are left with the problem of the educated public's estrangement from philosophy. If, on the other hand, philosophy is more broadly concerned with love and pursuit of wisdom as guidance for living, then we can profit from the lessons of sagacious basketball coaches by utilizing diverse methods. In his essay "The Present Dilemma in Philosophy," William James recalls remarks from a student's thesis in which the student expresses that he takes for granted that "when you entered a philosophic classroom you had to open relations with a universe entirely distinct from the one you left behind you in the street" (369). The problems of philosophers, historical or contemporary, tend not to be compelling to the majority of the population that may nevertheless be interested in acquiring wisdom pertaining to their lives and the world they live in.

If the job of philosophy is to relate wisdom in the art of living, then we must consider that literature and films are better suited to perform this work than abstract reasoning. It is not by accident that the French existentialists, in the aftermath of World War II, felt the need to move beyond discussions of abstractions and start writing short stories, novels, and plays to convey their ideas. Sartre described himself as primarily a writer, and confessed that he completed *Being and Nothingness* to gain credibility in the academic philosophical community. Sartre best expressed his philosophy within narrative structures that enabled him to place his characters in serious and difficult existential situations. Simone de Beauvoir contributed *The Ethics of Ambiguity* and *The Second Sex*, but directed most of her existentialist energy into novels. Albert Camus was unequivocal in his view about the superiority of literature over abstruse argumentation. He did not claim to be a philosopher and sometimes shunned the term, but he remarked, "People can think only in images. If you want to be a philosopher, write novels" (Camus, *Notebooks 1935–1942* 10).

Hard-boiled fiction and film noir are examples of the third option, all the more fascinating because their creators were not intentionally producing existential philosophy. A poor man's existentialism responds to the difficulties of living honorably in an immoral or amoral world, a persistent theme in moral and religious philosophy, and accomplishes this feat within the thrilling context of crime narratives. Noir does not present philosophical ideas in the form of technical argumentation but illustrates existential difficulties through the human drama of isolation, opaqueness, and meaninglessness. In hard-boiled fiction and film noir, events impose themselves, protagonists are forced to make choices, and those choices form and reveal character. Despite noir's deserved reputation for pessimism and its candid portrayals of human weakness, most protagonists ultimately act in ways meant to preserve their integrity and dignity even as they despairingly concede the insurmountable obstacles of their world. In a decayed society that does not reward honor, individuals attach special significance to acts they deem honorable. Philip Marlowe's episode with the diminutive Harry Jones illustrates his narrative and professional defense of the decent, little guy struggling to make an honest dollar in a dishonest and brutal world. Walter Neff and Jeff Bailey succumb to corruption that costs them their lives, but they leave honorable legacies through final acts of compassion for innocent bystanders caught in the crossfire of greed and deception. Why do they do so? We are not told what to think, but in a world without transcendent meaning or morality, protagonists appear to find personal meaning through professionalism and integrity and by garnering the respect of those whom they respect. A poor man's existentialism does not offer theoretical analysis of the metaphysical, epistemological, ethical, and political limitations of its world, but its protagonists express their answers in concrete situations with behavior and language that demonstrates respect for readers and viewers, and in turn, garners their respect.

The contrast between academic philosophy and hard-boiled fiction and film noir resembles and continues the conflict between Plato and the poets presented in *The Republic*. Plato was an aristocrat who lived during a period when the aristocratic system was in decline due to the appearance of a new merchant class and an early stage of democracy. The aristocratic virtues that Plato revered, which included the rights of the nobility, were under assault, and Plato believed the encroaching values of the vulgar were taught by those unscrupulous masters of rhetoric, the sophists. In order to undermine the sophists and defend aristocratic rule, Plato had to challenge the authority of Homer as well, for the poet's epics were instruments of education. Though Homer's dramas supported the virtues of the nobility, they did so, according to Plato, by appealing to the emotions and were not useful weapons in his war with the sophists. He needed to fight fire with fire, argument with argument. Plato intended to replace Homer's passionate appeal with a rational defense, and more generally, to supplant poetry with philosophy, as he defined it. By drawing a deep line in the sand between his methods and Homer's,

Plato maintains that philosophy involves protracted argumentation, and what Homer provides is something other than philosophy.

Plato may have placed his arguments in the context of drama as a concession to audiences accustomed to the poets, but the irony is that he evidently understood that these arguments do not develop in a vacuum and are not particularly compelling without the human concerns that give rise to the arguments. In his *Meditations*, Descartes places his thought experiment in a dramatic setting, explaining to his readers in plain language why he is moved to doubt his knowledge and suggesting why they should care about his enterprise. His process seems silly if it is performed without any motivation except for *the sake of knowledge*. As we move from the late eighteenth century, the period of Kant, to the beginning of the twentieth century, the dramatic context dissipates, and the arguments are presented as ends in themselves.

In the history of Western philosophy, Kant marks the beginning of the substantial movement toward professional concerns and technical language. His self-described Copernican revolution is an effort to overcome the problems of rationalist and empiricist thinkers. In other words, Kant engages the problems of philosophers, and his *Critique of Pure Reason* contains a plethora of his invented terms. As we have reviewed, the nineteenth century is remarkable for the fantastic systems of the German idealists, developed, at least initially, in response to Kant's conclusions. Their texts, especially Fichte's and Hegel's, present labyrinths of dialectical reasoning, as they attempt to describe reality as the self-unfolding of something called absolute reason. Positivists, such as the new realists and APA organizers, were among those who rebelled against the vision and methods of the metaphysical idealists. Throughout these years the conversation becomes increasingly restricted to internal disputes between professionals, and the quarrels involve matters of little interest to "outsiders." Plato's method of introducing his arguments in the context of practical concerns has largely been abandoned.

When the APA agrees that philosophy "should grapple only with problems of how implications between statements occur" (Holt et al. 21), it severs remaining ties to practical concerns. Since philosophical problems pertain only to the implications between statements, these statements are translated into the language of formal logic or symbolic logic. The English (or other) language components of the sentences are not needed and can only get in the way of the *legitimate* philosophical problems. Variables are substituted for the living issues imbedded in the statements' original language. For training purposes, philosophy students are required to solve logical problems that were never translated, meaning that they were given in symbolic form only. This practice implies that the practical concern is distracting and irrelevant. There is, one supposes, satisfaction to be gained by solving problems in formal logic, and logicians have been known to describe elaborate proofs as beautiful, but the interest for the nonprofessional is difficult to locate.

The creators of hard-boiled fiction and film noir are descendants of Greek dramatists, especially Aeschylus and Sophocles, in that they grapple with the metaphysical, epistemological, ethical, and political limitations of the world, instead of attempting to achieve certainty about the world through definition, analysis, and logic. There are some cultural differences between Greek drama and noir fiction, and the hard-boiled writers were resolved that their work should reflect "the world you live in," namely the United States during the early decades of the twentieth century. Given their concerns with the mystery of existence, it seems quite natural that hard-boiled fiction writers and noir directors found their niche in mystery fiction and film.

Just as Plato's attitudes about philosophy are realized through the academic philosophers, the existentialist stance of Greek drama finds its expression in hard-boiled fiction and film noir. The noir detective makes his first appearance in *Oedipus the King* and takes his final film bow in *Chinatown*. J. J. Gittes smirks when Evelyn Mulwray tells him that her husband believes he is an "innocent man." "I've been called a lot of things, Mrs. Mulwray, but never that," Gittes replies. Like Oedipus and his predecessors from the original film noir cycle, Gittes is not without sin, but he achieves tragic status despite his weakness and failure because his final actions are driven by honorable motives.

Furthermore, like Oedipus, Gittes did not heed Jocasta's warning that in a world filled with mystery there are many things we cannot know and things we are better off not knowing. Though *Chinatown* was released in 1974, it is set in Los Angeles during the 1930s, the period of hard-boiled fiction. Screenwriter Robert Towne found conditions strikingly similar to those in *Oedipus the King*, and his experience was the inspiration for *Chinatown*. Towne met a Hungarian cop who worked vice in Chinatown, and the cop remarked that his job consisted of doing "as little as possible." The cop explained to Towne that in Chinatown "you can't tell who is doing what to who. And you can't tell whether you're being asked to help prevent a crime, or you're inadvertently lending the color of the law to help commit a crime." Gittes was advised to do "as little as possible" by his superiors and is repeatedly warned off the Mulwray case. When his efforts lead to disaster and death, he can only mutter those words to himself, expressing that he, like Oedipus, failed to heed the wisdom he received.

The fact that Towne and the *Black Mask* writers were able to create their stories "right out of life" confirms that their narratives address existential concerns found in "the world you live in." Further confirmation is provided by the popularity and (belated) critical acceptance of hard-boiled fiction and film noir. A poor man's existentialism was set in the criminal world because conditions in that world are conducive to human drama and tragedy. Readers and viewers, though not themselves criminals, responded to these narratives, to the characters and situations, and to the practical philosophical issues they addressed. The concrete jungle, as these urban areas are called, effectively describes the rugged and tangled philosophical terrain these stories explore. A poor man's existentialism, in the forms of hard-boiled fiction and film noir, offered philosophy, so to speak, for the rest of us. Nevertheless, the interpretation of philosophy offered by the American Philosophical Association, the new realists, and the Harvard Philosophy Department effectively completed the work begun by Plato. In fact, it is rare to find a writer so much as mentioned in so-called comprehensive treatments of the history of Western philosophy. Professional philosophers of the period may have believed that they succeeded in reforming philosophy and that they rescued it from amateurs and the capacities of the vulgar. Though the philosophers successfully eliminated the writers from the field, by restricting themselves to the abstract problems of philosophers, they abandoned the traditional territory of philosophy and left space for the writers to take over the audience in search of wisdom as guidance for living.

ENDNOTES

1. This quote also appears in the film *The Maltese Falcon*.
2. The following critique of Socrates pertains to the character presented in Plato's dialogues, namely *The Republic*, the *Apology* and the *Euthyphro*.
3. For example, according to Socrates, a mathematician is not a mathematician when she or he makes an error.
4. Though Santayana contributed to this cooperative volume, he did not share this view.
5. *The Black Mask* was changed to *Black Mask*.
6. Shaw was a master swordsman. He won the national championship in sabers and the president's medal. He was an army captain and bayonet instructor during World War I, and he was called "Cap" by his *Black Mask* associates.
7. This dilemma also pertains to Continental philosophy, the twentieth century figures of which (e.g., Heidegger, Levinas, Derrida, etc.) offer idiosyncratic and obscure presentations.
8. This definition blessedly remains the first of eight offered in the *American Heritage Dictionary*.
9. It must be conceded that narratives can be as abstruse and obscure as technical prose. There are notable writers and directors, foreign and domestic, who specialize in these types of stories and films.

WORKS CONSULTED

Barnes, Hazel. *Humanistic Existentialism*. Lincoln: University of Nebraska, 1959. Print.

Barrett, William. *Irrational Man*. New York: Anchor, 1962. Print.

Borde, Raymond, and Etienne Chaumeton. *A Panorama of American Film Noir*. San Francisco: City Lights, 2002. Print.

Bubner, Rudiger, ed. *German Idealism*. New York: Penguin, 1997. Print.

Cain, James M. *Double Indemnity*. New York: Vintage Crime, 1992. Print.

———. *The Postman Always Rings Twice*. New York: Vintage Crime, 1992. Print.

Camus, Albert. *The Myth of Sisyphus*. New York: Vintage, 1991. Print.

———. *Notebooks: 1935–1942*. New York: Knopf, 1963. Print.

———. *The Plague*. New York: Vintage, 1988. Print.

———. *The Stranger*. New York: Vintage, 1991. Print.

Celine, Louis-Ferdinand. *Journey to the End of Night*. Cambridge, UK: Cambridge University Press, 1990. Print.

Chandler, Raymond. *The Big Sleep. Chandler: Stories and Early Novels*. Ed. Frank MacShane. New York: Library of America, 1995. 587–764. Print.

———. "The Simple Art of Murder." *Chandler: Later Novels and Other Writings*. New York: Library of America, 1995. 977–992. Print.

Christopher, Nicholas. *Somewhere in the Night: Film Noir & the American City*. New York: Owl, 1997. Print.

Conard, Mark T., ed. *The Philosophy of Film Noir*. Lexington: The University Press of Kentucky, 2006. Print.

Copjec, Joan. *Shades of Noir*. New York: Verso, 1993. Print.

Cotkin, George. *Existential America*. Baltimore: John Hopkins, 2003. Print.

Cruickshsank, John, ed. *The Novelist as Philosopher: Studies in French Fiction 1935–1960*. New York: Oxford University Press, 1962. Print.

Daly, Carroll John. *The Snarl of the Beast*. New York: Harpercollins, 1992. Print.

Davis, Mike. *City of Quartz*. New York: Vintage, 1992. Print.

Descartes, Rene. *Discourse on Method and The Meditations*. Trans. F. E. Sutcliffe. New York: Penguin, 1968. Print.

Dewey, John. "The Need for a Recovery of Philosophy." *Pragmatism: A Reader*. Ed. Louis Menard. New York: Vintage, 1997. 219–232. Print.

Dos Passos, John. *U.S.A.: The 42nd Parallel/1919/The Big Money*. New York: Library of America, 1995. Print.

Dostoevsky, Fyodor. *Notes from Underground*. New York: Vintage, 1994. Print.

Drake, Durant. "The Approach to Critical Realism." *Essays in Critical Realism*. New York: Gordian Press, 1968. 3–32. Print.

Dumenil, Lynn. *The Modern Temper*. New York: Hill and Wang, 1995. Print.

"Existentialism." Def. *The American Heritage Dictionary*. 3rd ed. 1992. Print.

Fearing, Kenneth. *The Big Clock. Crime Novels: American Noir of the 1930s & 1940s*. Ed. Robert Polito. New York: Library of America, 1997. 379–515. Print.

Fitzgerald, F. Scott. *This Side of Paradise*. New York: Scribner, 1960. Print.

Frohock, W. M. *The Novel of Violence in America*. Dallas: Southern Methodist University Press, 1957. Print.

Goodis, David. *Dark Passage*. London: Prion, 1999. Print.

Hammett, Dashiell. *Crime Stories & Other Writings*. New York: Library of America, 2001. Print.

———. *The Glass Key. Hammett: Complete Novels*. New York: Library of America, 1999. 587–777. Print.

———. *The Maltese Falcon. Hammett: Complete Novels*. New York: Library of America, 1999. 387–585. Print.

———. *Red Harvest. Hammett: Complete Novels*. New York: Library of America, 1999. 1–187. Print.

Hemingway, Ernest. *A Farewell to Arms*. New York: Scribner, 1995. Print.

———. *To Have and Have Not*. New York: Scribner, 1996. Print

———. *The Short Stories*. New York: Scribner, 1995. Print.

———. *The Sun Also Rises*. New York: Scribner, 1995. Print.

Himes, Chester. *If He Hollers Let Him Go*. New York: Thunder's Mouth Press, 2002. Print.

Holt, Edwin B., Walter T. Marvin, William Pepperell Montague, Ralph Barton Perry, Walter B. Pitkin, and Edward Gleason Spaulding. *The New Realism: Cooperative Studies in Philosophy*. New York: Mac-Millan, 1912. Print.

Horkheimer, Max, and Theodor Adorno. *Dialectic of Enlightenment*. New York: Continuum, 2002. Print.

Irwin, John T. *Unless the Threat of Death is Behind Them*. Baltimore: John Hopkins University Press, 2006. Print.

Jacoby, Russell. *Dogmatic Wisdom*. New York: Doubleday, 1994. Print.

———. *The Last Intellectuals*. New York: Basic Books, 1990. Print.

James, Williams. "The Present Dilemma in Philosophy." *The Writings of William James: A Comprehensive Edition*. Ed. John J. McDermott. Chicago: University of Chicago, 1977. 362–376. Print.

Jaspers, Karl. *Man in the Modern Age*. New York: Doubleday Anchor, 1957. Print.

Johnson, Kevin. *The Dark Page*. New Castle: Oak Knoll Press, 2007. Print.

Kafka, Franz. *The Trial*. New York: Schoken, 1995. Print.

Kaufmann, Walter. *Existentialism from Dostoevsky to Sartre*. New York: Meridan, 1975. Print.

Kierkegaard, Soren. *Fear and Trembling*. New York: Penguin, 1985. Print.

Kuklick, Bruce. *The Rise of American Philosophy*. New Haven: Yale University Press, 1977. Print.

Lachs, John. *The Relevance of Philosophy to Life*. Nashville: Vanderbit University Press, 1995. Print.

Leff, Leonard, and Jerrold L. Simmons. *The Dame in the Kimono: Hollywood Censorship and the Production Code from 1920–1960*. New York: Anchor, 1990. Print.

Lovejoy, Arthur. "Pragmatism Versus the Pragmatist." *Essays in Critical Realism*. New York: Gordian Press, 1968. 35–81. Print.

MacShane, Frank. *The Life of Raymond Chandler*. New York: Random House, 1976. Print.

Madden, David. *James M. Cain*. Boston: Twayne, 1970. Print.

———. *Tough Guy Writers of the Thirties*. Carbondale: Southern Illinois University, 1977. Print.

Marling, William. *The American Roman Noir*. Athens: University of Georgia, 1995. Print.

———. *Dashiell Hammett*. Boston: Twayne, 1983. Print.

———. *Raymond Chandler*. Boston: Twayne, 1986. Print.

Maurer, David. *The Big Con*. New York: Anchor, 1999. Print.

McCann, Sean. *Gumshoe America: Hard-boiled Crime Fiction and the Rise and Fall of New Deal Liberalism*. Durham: Duke University, 2000. Print.

McCoy, Horace. *They Shoot Horses Don't They? Crime Novels: American Noir of the 1930s & 1940s*. Ed. Robert Polito. 1997. 97–213. Print.

Metz, Christian. *The Imaginary Signifier: Psychoanalysis and the Cinema*. Bloomington: Indiana University Press, 1992. Print.

Mills, C. Wright. *The Power Elite*. New York: Oxford University, 1959. Print.

———. *White Collar*. New York: Oxford University, 1956. Print.

Motion Picture Producers and Distributors of America (MPPDA). *The Motion Picture Production Code*. David P. Hayes. 2000–2008. Web. 28 Oct. 2008. <http://productioncode.dhwritings.com/index.php>.

Naremore, James. *More Than Night*. Berkeley: University of California, 1998. Print.

Nietzshe, Friedrich. *Basic Writings of Nietzsche*. New York: Modern Library, 2000. Print.

———. *The Birth of Tragedy*. New York: Vintage, 1966. Print.

Nolan, William. *The Black Mask Boys*. New York: Morrow, 1985. Print.

O'Brien, Geoffrey. *Hardboiled America*. New York: Da Capo, 1997. Print.

Oliver, Kelly, and Benigno Trigo. *Noir Anxiety*. Minneapolis: University of Minnesota, 2003. Print.

Plato. *Apology*. Trans. G.M.A. Grube. *Complete Works*. Ed. John M. Cooper and D. S. Hutchinson. Indianapolis: Hackett, 1997. 17–36. Print.

———. *Parmenides*. Trans. Mary Louise Gill and Paul Ryan. *Complete Works*. Indianapolis: Hackett, 1997. 359–397. Print.

———. *The Republic*. Trans. Allan Bloom. 2nd ed. New York: Basic Books, 1991. Print.

"Philosophy." Def. 1. *The American Heritage Dictionary*. 3rd ed. 1992. Print.

Porfirio, Robert. "No Way Out: Existential Motifs in the Film Noir." *Film Noir Reader*. Ed. Alain Silver and James Ursini. New York: Limelight, 1995. 76–93. Print.

Riesman, David. *The Lonely Crowd*. New Haven: Yale University, 1989. Print.

Sante, Luc. *Low Life*. New York: Vintage, 1992. Print.

Sartre, Jean-Paul. *Being and Nothingness*. New York: Washington Square, 1984. Print.

———. *Existentialism and Human Emotions*. New York: Citadel, 1987. Print.

———. *Nausea*. New York: New Directions, 1964. Print.

———. "Situation of the Writer in 1947." *What is Literature?* New York: Philosophical Library, 1949. 161–297. Print.

Schrader, Paul. "Notes on Film Noir." *Film Noir Reader*. Ed. Alain Silver and James Ursini. New York: Limelight, 1995. 52–63. Print.

Schulberg, Budd. *What Makes Sammy Run?* New York: Vintage, 1993. Print.

Silver, Alain, and Margaret Ward. *Film Noir Encyclopedia*. New York: Overlook, 1979. Print.

Silver, Alain, and James Ursini. *Film Noir Reader 2*. New York: Limelight, 1999. Print.

———. *Film Noir Reader 4*. New York: Limelight, 2004. Print.

Smith, Erin. *Hard-Boiled: Working-Class Readers and Pulp Magazines*. Philadelphia: Temple University, 2000. Print.

Sperber, A. M., and Lax, Eric. *Bogart*. New York: Morrow, 1997. Print.

Spillane, Mickey. *The Mike Hammer Collection*. Vol. 1. New York: New American Library, 2001. Print.

———. *The Mike Hammer Collection*. Vol. 2. New York: New American Library, 2001. Print.

Telotte, J. P. *Voices in the Dark: The Narrative Patterns of Film Noir*. Chicago: University of Illinois, 1989. Print.

Thompson, Jim. *The Killer Inside Me*. New York: Vintage Crime, 1991. Print.

Tuska, Jon. *Dark Cinema*. Westport: Greenwood Press, 1984. Print

Whyte, William. *The Organization Man*. New York: Simon and Schuster, 1956. Print.

Wild, John. *The Challenge of Existentialism*. Bloomington: Indiana University, 1966. Print.

Wilder, Billy. Interview by Robert Porfirio. *Film Noir Reader 3*. New York: Limelight, 2002. 100–119. Print.

Wilshire, Bruce. *The Moral Collapse of the University*. New York: New York University Press, 1990. Print.

Woolrich, Cornell. *I Married a Dead Man*. *Crime Novels: American Noir of the 1930s & 1940s*. Ed. Robert Polito. New York: Library of America, 1997. 797–973. Print.

Selected Filmography

Angel Face. Dir. Otto Preminger. RKO, 1952. Film.

The Asphalt Jungle. Dir. John Huston. MGM, 1950. Film.

The Big Clock. Dir. John Farrow. Universal, 1948. Film.

The Big Combo. Dir. Joseph H. Lewis. Allied Artists, 1955. Film.

The Big Heat. Dir. Fritz Lang. Columbia, 1953. Film.

The Big Knife. Dir. Robert Aldrich. United Artists, 1955. Film.

The Big Sleep. Dir. Howard Hawks. Warner Bros, 1946. Film.

Black Angel. Dir. Roy William Neill. Universal, 1946. Film.

Body and Soul. Dir. Robert Rossen. Enterprise, 1947. Film.

Born to Kill. Dir. Robert Wise. RKO, 1947. Film.

Brute Force. Dir. Jules Dassin. Universal, 1947. Film.

Chinatown. Dir. Roman Polanski. Paramount, 1974. Film.

Cornered. Dir. Edward Dmytryk. RKO, 1945. Film.

Criss Cross. Dir. Robert Siodmak. Universal, 1949. Film.

D. O. A. Dir. Rudolph Mate. United Artists, 1950. Film.

Dark Passage. Dir. Delmer Daves. Warner Bros., 1947. Film.

Detour. Dir. Edgar Ulmer. PRC, 1945. Film.

Double Indemnity. Dir. Billy Wilder. Paramount, 1944. Film.

The Fallen Sparrow. Dir. Richard Wallace. RKO, 1943. Film.

The File on Thelma Jordan. Dir. Robert Siodmak. Paramount, 1949. Film.

Force of Evil. Dir. Abraham Polonsky. Enterprise, 1949. Film.

The Glass Key. Dir. Stuart Heisler. Paramount, 1942. Film.

Gun Crazy. Dir. Joseph H. Lewis. United Artists, 1949. Film.

He Walked by Night. Dir. Alfred Werker. Eagle-Lion, 1949. Film.

High Sierra. Dir. Raoul Walsh. Warner Bros., 1940. Film.

In a Lonely Place. Dir. Nicholas Ray. Columbia, 1950. Film.

Kansas City Confidential. Dir. Phil Karlson. United Artists, 1952. Film.

Key Largo. Dir. John Huston. Warner Bros., 1948. Film.

The Killers. Dir. Robert Siodmak. Universal, 1946. Film.

The Killing. Dir. Stanley Kubrick. United Artists, 1956. Film.

Kiss Me Deadly. Dir. Robert Aldrich. United Artists, 1955. Film.

Kiss Tomorrow Goodbye. Dir. Gordon Douglas. Warner Bros., 1950. Film.

The Lady from Shanghai. Dir. Orson Welles. Columbia, 1948. Film.

Laura. Dir. Otto Preminger. 20th Century Fox, 1944. Film.

The Maltese Falcon. Dir. John Huston. Warner Bros., 1941. Film.

Murder, My Sweet. Dir. Edward Dmytryk. RKO, 1944. Film.

The Narrow Margin. Dir. Richard Fleischer. RKO, 1952. Film.

Night and the City. Dir. Jules Dassin. 20th Century Fox, 1950. Film.

Nightmare Alley. Dir. Edmund Golding. 20th Century Fox, 1947. Film.

Odds Against Tomorrow. Dir. Robert Wise. United Artists, 1959. Film.

Out of the Past. Dir. Jacques Tourneur. RKO, 1947. Film.

Phantom Lady. Dir. Robert Siomak. RKO, 1944. Film.

The Pitfall. Dir. Andre de Toth. United Artists, 1948. Film.

Plunder Road. Dir. Hubert Cornfield. Regal Films, 1957. Film.

The Postman Always Rings Twice. Dir. Tay Garnett. MGM, 1947. Film.

Private Hell 36. Dir. Don Siegel. Filmakers, 1954. Film.

Pulp Fiction. Dir. Quentin Tarentino, Miramax, 1994. Film.

Raw Deal. Dir. Anthony Mann. Eagle-Lion, 1948. Film.

Roadblock. Dir. Harold Daniels. RKO, 1951. Film.

Scarlet Street. Dir. Fritz Lang. Universal, 1945. Film.

The Set-Up. Dir. Robert Wise. RKO, 1949. Film.

Sorry, Wrong Number. Dir. Anatole Litvak. Paramount, 1948. Film.

Stranger on the Third Floor. Dir. Boris Ingster. RKO, 1940. Film.

Sunset Boulevard. Dir. Billy Wilder. Paramount, 1950. Film.

Sweet Smell of Success. Dir. Alexander Mackendrick. United Artists, 1957. Film.

T-Men. Dir. Anthony Mann. Eagle-Lion, 1947. Film.

They Live by Night. Dir. Nicholas Ray. RKO, 1948. Film.

They Won't Believe Me. Dir. Irving Pichel. RKO, 1947. Film.

This Gun for Hire. Dir. Frank Tuttle. Paramount, 1942. Film.

Touch of Evil. Dir. Orson Welles. Universal-International, 1949. Film.

Where Danger Lives. Dir. John Farrow. RKO, 1950. Film.

White Heat. Dir. Raoul Walsh. Warner Bros., 1949. Film.

The Woman in the Window. Dir. Fritz Lang. RKO, 1944. Film.

INDEX